Run to Win!

SUCCESS SERIES – BOOK ONE

Run to Win!

Christine Caine

New Wine Press

New Wine Ministries
PO Box 17
Chichester
West Sussex
United Kingdom
PO19 2AW

ISBN 978-1-903725-79-5

Typeset by CRB Associates, Reepham, Norfolk
Cover design by CCD, www.ccdgroup.co.uk
Printed in the United States of America

Contents

A note from your coach

Not many people know that God loves running. Even if you have not seen Him out jogging recently, take my word for it, He is into running in a big way! This book is all about running – running the race of your life, running it well and finishing strong. The Bible uses the metaphor of a race to describe the Christian life: *"You've all been to the stadium and seen the athletes race. Everyone runs; one wins. Run to win"* (1 Corinthians 9:24a MSG). Our life has a start and a finish, a clear goal to aim for. How we run our race to get from the start to the finish is critically important. As you read on, the reason for this will become clear. I hope that you will learn some important principles that will enable you to run a great race – to live a life marked by passion and purpose.

I believe that God has created every person to be a winner in the race of life. That includes you and me – no exceptions. But what does it mean to win in life? Does winning mean having a great job, a big house, a huge salary, a gorgeous wife/handsome, dynamic husband? Is it all about being a high achiever? No!

You may have any or all of the above and still not be a winner in life! "Really?" I hear you say. Yes, it's true. Running a great race in life is simply this: *it is being who God created you to be and doing all that God created you to do.* Winning is about fulfilling your God-given purpose and destiny in Christ.

I have studied the art and technique of running (yes, there is both an art and a technique), and I have realised that many of these principles can be applied to our spiritual lives. I have written this book with the intention of putting into your hands an easy-to-read, concise, practical, inspirational and motivational tool that will help you to win in every aspect of your life: spiritually, emotionally, relationally, financially and physically. Throughout

> **Winning is about fulfilling your God-given purpose and destiny in Christ.**

this book, strategically placed "checkpoints" will recap the important principles you have learned. I encourage you to pace yourself so that you allow time to strengthen, recharge and evaluate yourself at each checkpoint. I hope you are equipped and empowered to "run to win".

Chris

PART 1

Runners Take Your Mark

The marathon begins...

I love all things Greek! I guess that's why I love to run.
Running has been a part of Greek culture for a long,
long time. The Greeks invented marathon running and
this is how it happened (bear with me while I indulge
in a short history lesson): In 490 BC, there was a
famous battle between the Greek and Persian armies
called the Battle of Marathon. King Darius I of Persia
was trying to conquer the Greeks in order to expand
his already vast empire. But despite the fact that they
were outnumbered four to one, the Greeks refused to
be beaten. (We don't go down easy!) At one critical
point in the battle, the Greeks launched an almost
suicidal surprise attack that was to prove pivotal. By
the end of the battle, six thousand Persians lay dead
while the Greeks had lost fewer than two hundred men.
The surviving Persians fled back to their ships and the
Greeks secured their homeland!

According to legend, a Greek soldier by the name
of Pheidippides (try saying his name really quickly)
was chosen to take news of the victory back to
Athens. In order to do this, he had to run from the

town of Marathon – a distance of approximately twenty-one miles. Legend has it that he never slowed down once. He had been fighting all day and he pushed himself beyond all normal limits of endurance to run this great distance. Entering Athens, he shouted, "We are victorious!" and then he literally dropped dead!

This heroic act inspired the modern marathon race. At first, the intention was to retrace Pheidippides' original course, but its popularity has meant that marathons now take place all over the world. The marathon became a competitive race when Michel Bréal put the event on the programme of the first ever modern Olympic Games held in Athens in 1896. Interestingly, this first ever marathon was won by Spiros Louis, a Greek shepherd, who completed the course in two hours and fifty-eight minutes, despite stopping on the way to drink a glass of wine provided by his uncle who was waiting for him at the village of Chalandri! Funnily enough, chasing sheep and drinking wine has not been a feature of subsequent marathon training programmes!

The Christian life is more like a marathon than a sprint

You may be wondering why I have just spent the first few paragraphs of this book giving you a brief history lesson about the origins of the marathon? I did that because I believe that there is a powerful, spiritual lesson to be learned from our friend Pheidippides. Some historians suggest that he might have actually lived if he had done a few things differently. Instead of pacing himself for marathon distance, he ran the entire course as if he was running a short sprint. If he had slowed down a little, stopped occasionally and taken a drink and some food, in addition to tempering his speed on the gruelling uphill stretches, it is possible that he could have lived. Similarly, the Christian life is much more a marathon than it is a sprint. God wants us to be endurance runners – the kind of people who will run the whole stretch of our race and finish victorious at the end. That being so, it is important that we learn to pace ourselves.

Remember what Paul said about running to win in the race of life? He then goes on to say,

> *"You've all been to the stadium and seen the athletes race. Everyone runs; one wins. Run to win. All good athletes train hard. They do it for a gold medal that tarnishes and fades. You're after one that's gold eternally. I don't know about you, but I'm running hard for the finish line. I'm giving it everything I've got. No sloppy living for me! I'm staying alert and in top condition. I'm not going to get caught napping, telling everyone else all about it and then missing out myself."*
>
> (1 Corinthians 9:24–27, MSG)

Paul emphasises the importance of *training* and *discipline.* His vivid description of running to win in life inspired me to do some research on what makes a marathon runner tick. I studied their preparation, their training techniques, mental attitudes and lots of other aspects of running. (Admittedly, I did not initially realise there were so many aspects to running!) I discovered that the very principles that are foundational for running a marathon in the natural are equally applicable to running our spiritual race.

Some will say, "I can't be bothered with training," because they prefer to just get out there and run without going through the preparation process. But good preparation and technique are vital if you want to actually reach the finish line. As I continue to run my own race, I am aware of the fact that many people who started this faith adventure with me have dropped out of their race. The absence of disciplined training in their lives meant that they didn't have the spiritual stamina to keep going when the going got tough. Instead of running to win, they have been defeated by disappointment, discouragement, distraction, disillusionment or disease, and because of this, they have dropped out of the race.

I believe that if we apply the truths in this book to our Christian lives, we will not only get to the finish line, but we will win in life. Training and discipline in the race of life mean making the right choices today to ensure that we run to win. Don't allow yourself to be forced out of your race by poor preparation and training. Apply the principles in the following runner's training guide.

The Spiritual Marathon Runner's Training Guide

1. A marathon runner has a vision for the whole race

An experienced marathon runner will have visualised their whole race – the entire 26.3 miles from start to finish – *before* they set off. Long-distance runners get to grips with the race *internally*, in their heart, before ever setting foot on the course. Whilst it is not possible for someone to visualise every inch of the course in detail (unless they have a photographic memory), a runner can mentally prepare for the fact that there will be bends and curves, there will be uphill and downhill stretches, there will be times they want to give up, and there will be times of extreme fatigue where every inch of their body wants to stop running. Runners prepare themselves mentally so that they are not caught out by these changes in the landscape when they occur. The visualisation process empowers them for what lies ahead.

We need to have that same overall sense of *vision* for every area of our lives. Having a clear picture of what the race of life is all about, where we are heading, and what we are likely to encounter along the way will sustain us for the entire duration. Keeping the end in sight will help us keep going when things are tough – when we are struggling over rough terrain or labouring up hills. Proverbs 29:18 in the King James Version says, *"Where there is no vision, the people perish."* Many people do not finish their race simply through a lack of long-term vision. At the first sign of opposition, difficulty or adversity, they simply give up.

Whilst having a vision for our lives is critical, it does not immunise us against the obstacles and pitfalls that will inevitably crop up. In life, things we don't like happen! It's just a fact and there is nothing we can do about it. John 16:33 states, *"I have told you these things, so that in me you may have peace. In this world you will have trouble. But take heart! I have overcome the world"* (NIV).

> **Many people do not finish their race simply through a lack of long-term vision.**

Jesus made it clear that trials will come in life, but we do not have to drop out of the race because of them. By maintaining our vision, we can stay on track. I have encountered many trials and challenges in my race thus far (and I'm sure there are many more ahead).

One of the first real challenges that I encountered in my own marathon came when I made the decision to enrol in Bible school in order to begin to move forward in my calling. Not only was this something that no one in my family had ever done, but it was also generally frowned upon by the wider community of which I was a part. I had to stand alone in this decision and remain steadfast in my convictions even though everyone whom I loved and cared about had removed their support from my life. The pressure was so intense during this time that I almost gave up, but the vision that God had placed in my heart sustained me. I knew then that God's plan for my life was to preach all over the world and see lives transformed by the power of the Gospel. It was the presence of long-term vision that helped me endure that very difficult season in my life.

Another area in which I had to ensure I kept a long-term vision was when it came to dating and the possibility of marriage. When I was in my late twenties and single, I had a vision for the kind of man I wanted to marry. I wanted a man who was passionate about fulfilling the purpose of God, who loved the house of God, and would be a great husband and father. (I definitely got all that and more in my husband, Nick.) This vision stopped me from settling for just any relationship and enabled me to keep waiting patiently for the "God one". There are so many people who sabotage their destiny in this area of life, because they do not trust God to bring the right partner along. Instead, due to fear of being left alone, or sheer desperation, they end up settling for less than God's best in the short term, which often has negative ramifications in the long term.

Another area that has required me to have a long-term vision is that of health and fitness. I gave birth to my second daughter, Sophia, at thirty-nine years of age and am very aware that I will be sixty at her twenty-first birthday party. It is the vision of me being not only *present*, but fit and healthy at Sophia's twenty-first that keeps me going to the gym every morning. Each time I am tempted to sleep in (which is most mornings!), I keep the vision of the future before me which enables me to overcome the temptation of putting my head back down on the pillow. That is the motivating factor that keeps me working out and maintaining a healthy diet.

Check point 1

Pause for a moment and reflect on the following: are there any areas in your life where you have given up because you've lost sight of the bigger picture, or lost your vision for the whole race? Maybe you have stalled in your spiritual life and you are no longer moving forward. Maybe you have lost your vision for life emotionally, physically, relationally or financially.

If so, identify the point at which you gave up, renew your vision, and pick up the pace again. Remember, in order to have the right perspective, you need to:

- Visualise the whole race
- Be ready for challenges
- Be patient!

2. A marathon runner has a commitment to preparation

In order to run a marathon, a person has to be thoroughly prepared. Otherwise, not only will they fail to complete the course but they will do their body some serious damage. Marathon runners who are not adequately prepared are known to have suffered from numerous complaints including tendonitis, shin splints, hamstring pulls and tears, and a multitude of back problems. Osteopaths tell us that all of these can be prevented by a preparation programme that includes the correct stretching and muscle balancing exercises, plus a well-paced running-training regime, and even something as simple as wearing the right gear.

It is evident that preparation is crucial before a runner ever sets foot on a course. The celebrated marathon runner Tom Fleming made a statement which has become a training motto for the Boston marathon (the oldest modern-day marathon and hailed as one of the toughest and greatest races in the world): "Somewhere in the world, someone is training when you are not. When you race him, he will win."[1] A friend of mine from Canada wanted to run in the Boston Marathon and once he had decided he was going to do it, he had to embark on a *two-year* preparation programme to get his body ready for the race! Most marathon running coaches recommend a minimum of six months training before attempting a marathon – and only then if you are really experienced. Even seasoned runners have to have a long build-up to a marathon in order to finish the course on race day.

In reality, many people who sign up for long-distance races drop out long before the starting gun is ever fired. Their intentions are admirable, but a weakness of commitment results in a weakness of preparation. When it comes to race day, they are unprepared and uncertain as to whether they can make it, so they withdraw and don't compete. Juma Ikangaa, the winner of the 1989 New York marathon summed it up when he said, "The will to win means nothing if you haven't the will to prepare."[2]

A weakness of commitment results in a weakness of preparation.

Most of us prefer instant results to having to go through a preparation process. When things don't happen as quickly as we would like, we tend to give up or drop out. How many diets have we started and never finished? How many New Year's resolutions have we made and never followed through with? How many books have we bought and never read? The list could go on and on.

We are often guilty of "talking a great game" and then not following through with our actions. Lip service and heart commitment are two very different things! For the runner, there must be an absolute commitment to training in order to sacrifice the time needed to discipline, test and strengthen the mind and body. It is the same for us in our spiritual life. We have to lay a foundation that will support us in the future.

Even though one of my primary gifts is that of preaching and teaching, I rarely ever preached when I was a youth leader in my local youth ministry. During that season of my life, I served the youth ministry by using my car to drive young people to youth meetings, setting up the youth auditorium, vacuuming the floor, cleaning the toilets and doing whatever else needed to be done. Although I had a dream and a desire in my heart to preach all over the world, I knew that God needed to do a deep work *in* me so that He could do a great work *through* me in the future. (I share this story extensively in my book, *A Life Unleashed*.) Although I found this preparation phase incredibly frustrating, lonely and sometimes tedious, I know that if I had not stayed committed to the preparation process during those years, I would not be doing what I'm doing today.

The Bible records the fact that a man called Elisha arose to become one of the most outstanding prophets of God ever to walk the earth. He followed in the footsteps of his mentor, Elijah, and his life was marked by faithfulness. Elisha went on to become twice as powerful as Elijah – to have a "double anointing" to put it in Bible language – and the key to his success was *preparation.*

In 1 Kings 19:21 we read the simple yet telling statement, *"*[Elisha] *arose and followed Elijah, and became his servant."* During the early years of his preparation for ministry, Elisha just served Elijah. That was it! "Go and get that for me," Elijah would say and Elisha would go. "Do this for me..." and he would do it. There was not necessarily a "please" or "thank you". Elisha just got on with it. I guess he had seen something in his future that God wanted to do and decided that cooperation was the best policy. While he was busy serving, God was grooming him for greatness, whether he realised it or not. God was shaping and moulding him for future effectiveness. If he cooperated with God's training programme, he was sure to be in the right place at the right time when his promotion was due.

Many people are not where they are supposed to be when it comes time for God to promote them, simply because they have not been committed to preparation. As a result, they miss out on or defer the progress of their destiny. We live in a culture that places no value on the anonymity of preparation. Instead of understanding that it is a vital part of our overall journey, people always look for a shortcut! But preparation is essential if God is going to make us into who we need to be so that we can do what we're called to do.

In 2 Kings 2:14 we read about the moment when it came time for Elisha to be released into his destiny. He *"took the mantle of Elijah that had fallen from him."* It turned out that timing and position were absolutely vital to the fulfilment of Elisha's destiny. If he had not been fully committed to serving Elijah and had not doggedly pursued him (even when Elijah tried to get rid of him, as you will find if you read the whole story) then he would not have been in the right place at the right time to take up the mantle of Elijah. This proves that *what you do in your preparation time will determine your destiny.* Everything matters. We have to learn not to devalue any part of the preparation process because every part is important.

Check point 2

Many marathon runners testify to the fact that most of their time is spent in preparation. Dave Bedford, an English distance runner who was known to occasionally put in 200 miles per week in training said, "Running is a lot like life. Only 10% of it is exciting. 90% of it is slog." Preparation can be really hard work, but every aspect of it is important. It is usually the things we do behind the scenes when others don't see us that determine our destiny.

- If you are thoroughly prepared, you will complete your course.
- Always cooperate and stay faithful to God's preparation process in your life.
- Like Elisha, being constantly ready and prepared will position you to reach your destiny.

3. A marathon runner endures discomfort and pain

Sir Roger Bannister, the first man to break the elusive four-minute-mile barrier, once said, "The man who can drive himself further once the effort gets painful is the man who will win."[3] No challenge in life is easy or else it wouldn't be a challenge! The fact is that running the race of the Christian life is a *big* challenge. Sometimes it hurts and we have to get used to that. The painful times are the times when we most need to fall back on our earlier preparation and training to get us through.

> **No challenge in life is easy or else it wouldn't be a challenge!**

My friend Mike, who has run several marathons, says that he regularly puts up with aching joints, sore muscles, powerful cramps, sore feet and an aching back during a race. I asked him, "Why on earth would you want to endure such pain and discomfort?" He answered, "Chris, it's just part of running a marathon and if you want to finish you have to press past the pain barrier."

I have discovered that if we are going to run our race and finish our course, we are going to have to keep pressing beyond what is comfortable. Isaiah 54:2 says,

> *"Enlarge the place of your tent,*
> *And let them stretch out the curtains of your*
> *   dwellings;*
> *Do not spare;*
> *Lengthen your cords,*
> *And strengthen your stakes."*

In this passage, God is saying to us, in effect, "I cannot fit what I want to do in your life in the space that you have. You are not thinking, believing, imagining or dreaming big enough! I need you to get bigger so that I can do what I want to do through you." The four words that God then uses to describe how this "getting bigger" will happen imply anything but comfort. These words are *enlarge, stretch, lengthen* and *strengthen.* Every one of these involves growth, pain and discomfort, but it is worth the effort.

Enlarge

In the same way that a runner needs to enlarge his/her muscles in order to exceed their previous capabilities as an athlete, when we allow God to use our circumstances to enlarge our perspective of Him, our inward capacity to live out our calling increases. When our view of God is expanded we gain the confidence to trust Him for more and we can believe Him to do bigger, more expansive things in and through our lives than ever before. This expansion gives us the understanding that God is strategic when positioning His people in both place and circumstance. What once seemed like an unattainable goal or an impossible task now appears possible, because our perspective of God is so much bigger.

Much like the way a runner uses physical training to build stamina, Christians must use spiritual training to enlarge their personal capacity to trust in God. It's a runner's strict day-to-day training regime that enables him/her to run longer, faster, further and with unstoppable force on the day of the race. In the marathon of life this is what we need to do in order to run to win.

Stretch

Whilst writing this book, I was inspired to go out for a run. I switched off my laptop, went out and did a fantastic 10km run (even I was impressed with myself!). When I got home, my daughter Catherine met me at the door, eager to show me her new trampoline. Instead of doing my usual "warm down" stretching routine, I went with her straight away. Three hours later, I couldn't move. Of course, my fingers were OK, so I kept on writing, but if I stood up to go to the bathroom (which is frequently after two children), I needed wheelchair assistance to get there. My leg muscles had seized up. Yes, you guessed it – I should have stretched!

If we don't allow ourselves to be continually stretched beyond our current limits In life, we will get tight and seize up. Once that has happened, we will no longer be able to run effectively. Many people are no longer running to win simply because they stopped stretching. They became inflexible to new thoughts, ideas and enterprises. They weren't prepared to endure short-term discomfort for long-term gain.

In order to continue running my course in life, I have often had to stretch beyond where I felt comfortable and keep pressing forward. As a youth leader, I began by supervising a small group of six girls and, at the time, that was a stretch for me. After a while, I decided to get out of my comfort zone and accept the challenge of leading a larger group. When I made that transition, it stretched me to the max, but I was later able to allow God to stretch me again, and then again, until I was leading a state-wide youth movement with thousands of young people. God has now given me the privilege of leading an international ministry and mission initiative to Europe. This wouldn't have been possible if I had not been stretched.

Lengthen

I've been working with a physiotherapist for the past few months because I damaged my hip flexor when I was younger (did you even know you had one of these?). Through years of not stretching properly after running, the muscles in my hip flexor and glutes totally seized up and stopped working properly. As a result, they were causing me quite a bit of pain. By being disciplined and getting help, my hip flexor muscle has now lengthened. But the lengthening has only come through consistent stretching. Well, the physiotherapist called it stretching. I called it torture and agony!

To lengthen is to go further in your output and effort, because if we do not continue to "lengthen", we cannot run to win. Promotion in life does not come from doing the bare minimum. Look at the type of people who are promoted in the workplace compared to those who don't get promoted. It is the extra effort that they put in that makes them winners.

I am often asked why it seems that some people succeed in life and have their dreams fulfilled and others don't. Does God have favourites? I don't think so. I believe that as sons and daughters of the King, we are all God's favourites. The truth is, those who are prepared to press in and lengthen are the ones who win in life; but putting in that extra effort is a conscious choice that we have to make. Even in writing this book, I have had to make a concerted effort to increase my output. In the midst of returning from a missions trip, having lots of work to catch up on in the office, looking after two toddlers and having a full-on church life, I had a decision to make: I could grumble and complain about my workload or I could choose to go further and increase my output to complete this project that God put on my heart. You are now holding in your hands the fruit of the decision that I made.

> **It is the extra effort that they put in that makes them winners.**

Strengthen

After yet another session with Darren (the physiotherapist/torturer), he told me that the next phase of my treatment would be to strengthen my lower back because it affects what happens in my hip and in my leg. He told me that if I want to keep running, and in the future walking (which is very high on my list of priorities!), I have to strengthen those muscles. My muscles have to get stronger if they are to have the capacity to handle the demands of my life. You guessed it: this means more discomfort and more pain as I diligently go to the gym and lift weights to strengthen my lower back muscles!

In the same way, we need to have spiritual strength and stamina if we are to run our race and reach the finish line in one piece. And the only way to increase your spiritual strength is to give your inner man a regular workout at the spiritual gym! See the next section on daily disciplines to find out how to do that. The only way to increase our strength is by lifting heavier and heavier weights. By doing this, we increase our capacity to "load bear". As a result, when challenges in life come, be they spiritual, emotional, physical, financial or relational, we will have the grit and determination to overcome them and keep running.

Check point 3

Every runner who is committed to a long-distance race knows that that race will involve pain and discomfort. Runners endure the pain for the thrill of winning, of crossing the finish line having completed the course. Peter Maher, an Olympic sub 2:12 marathon runner said, "Running is a big question mark that's there each and every day. It asks you, 'Are you going to be a wimp or are you going to be strong today?'" Life asks us the same question regarding our spiritual race: are we going to quit for the sake of avoiding a bit of pain and discomfort, or will we press through to the end? Make a choice and move forward!

- Understand you will need to learn to endure discomfort and pain.
- Make a decision to cooperate with God's programme to enlarge, stretch, lengthen and strengthen you.
- God has no favourites – everyone is born to win.

4. A marathon runner maintains daily disciplines

Paul said, *"I discipline my body and bring it into subjection, lest, when I have preached to others, I myself should become disqualified"* (1 Corinthians 9:27).

Day in and day out, marathon runners have to be disciplined people. They train whatever the weather conditions and despite everything else they have going on in their lives. For example, my friend Mike lives in Alberta, Canada. In the winter he gets up at 3:30am (and their winter temperatures can be minus 20) in order to fit in a two and a half hour run before work. He never gets up and says to himself, "It's too cold today and I've got a busy day ahead. I think I'll go back to bed!" (although he might think that). Whether he feels like it or not, he understands that if he wants to be ready to run the marathon on race day, he must exercise the daily discipline of running. Just because he lives in Canada and is subject to the weather conditions there does not mean that he is exempt from doing what everyone else does in order to participate in the marathon.

People often say to me, "Gee, I would love to do what you're doing, Christine. I would love to travel and preach the Gospel." But rarely do I ever see these same people follow through and do anything about their desire. It takes a great deal of sacrifice and discipline to fulfil the purpose of God. I travel frequently with my family and just to get to a city to preach is a feat of incredible planning, co-ordination and discipline. Can you imagine flying over twenty-four hours across time zones with two children under *five, every month*? In order to write this book, I have to wake up before my girls (which is very early!) and write after they have gone to bed. I have discovered that the perfect time to do anything does not just happen, it comes from exercising consistent daily discipline.

Many people want to stand on the winning podium of life, but not everyone is prepared to maintain the daily disciplines required to get them there. Not every waking moment of our marathon is glamorous, nor is it absent of sacrifice, dedication and consistency. In the midst of the excitement of seeing our God-given dream realised, we must remember that there is always a price to be paid.

Unwavering commitment to preparation and training is a major determinant of how successful we will be in the marathon of life. Training is essential because it not only strengthens our physical capacity, but it also prepares us for possible obstacles and hindrances that we may encounter along the way.

Just as marathon runners are constantly in training, Christians are constantly in training too. Every day, we need to make the effort to do the things that will determine our level of success in the future. These daily disciplines include: reading the

Bible, prayer, waiting on God, praise and worship, and asking God to fill us afresh with the Holy Spirit.

We will look at each of these disciplines in more detail in the next section of the book. For now, remember: *it is the small, seemingly insignificant things we do every day that determine whether we will win or lose in life.*

Athletes cannot live however they want and expect to be in peak condition for racing. They have to follow a tightly disciplined regime. It's exactly the same in our spiritual lives. God has given us moral guidelines for living life and certain spiritual disciplines that we need to maintain in order to win in life. We must keep up those disciplines in order to keep our spiritual lives on track. It seems as though the longer we walk with God, the more we let the small things slip. Endurance is built by paying attention to the small things. The simple disciplines of the faith are ones that no Christian ever outgrows. They may appear boring and mundane to some but they are actually the invisible force that is continually moving us forward in the purposes of God.

It is these basic spiritual disciplines that have kept me on course and running my race for the last twenty years. Just doing the basics is enough to keep you on track! You don't need a dozen prophetic words from a dozen different people to remind you what you're supposed to be doing. Being intentional about walking with God day by day will do it. Keep doing the simple things and you will not wander off the track of your destiny.

The author Graham Cooke has suggested that we should live in "day-tight compartments". In other words, take one day at a time and seek to keep the simple disciplines going. That way, one day will lead to the next day, the next week, the next year and eventually a lifetime. When it comes to discipline, it is just easier to think of one day at a time! I know that if I did not live a disciplined life, it wouldn't matter how much I prayed, fasted, confessed or believed, I would not be running to win. It is making the right choice with every moment that we have in our hand that determines our destiny. Daily disciplines may not seem glamorous, but they provide us with the foundation to do what we need to do in the future.

Robert de Castella, the famous Australian marathon runner of the 1980s said, "A lot of people do not realise that about 98% of the running I put in is anything but glamorous. It is 2% joyful participation and 98% dedication." The same is true in our spiritual lives.

Check point 4

I was twenty-five years old when I decided to start running. I thought that it would be easy. I was ready to run a marathon. I had all the proper gear and looked like a professional as I left my house. After less than one minute

(I am not joking!), I yelled to my friend, "Please, call an ambulance, I'm having a heart attack!" I sat in the gutter and waited to die. I could have easily given up at that moment and never run again. The next day I had a choice: would I run or not? It was that simple. The next day, I lasted perhaps ninety seconds instead of sixty, and then five minutes, and then fifteen. These days, I sometimes feel like Forrest Gump – I could run forever! But if I hadn't made the decision to keep up with my daily disciplines, I would never have broken through to be where I am now. Someone once said, "We are what we do continuously, hence, excellence is not an act but a habit."

- Good marathon runners keep up a disciplined training regime whether they feel like it or not. We need to do the same to keep our spiritual lives on track.
- Everything you do in one area of life affects all the other areas of your life.
- Focus on one day at a time and remember that the small, seemingly insignificant things count!

5. A marathon runner focuses on the goal

One factor that is critical in helping a runner to maintain focus right to the end of their race is keeping the end in sight. Experienced marathon runners are focused solely on crossing the finishing line. Their objective is nothing less than completion. As my friend Kylie always says, "Christine, I have one goal and that's just to finish the race. I put my head down and keep going with the intention of finishing. I don't care who passes me or what else is going on; I'm just going to finish."

The apostle Paul exemplified this attitude of running to finish his race. In Philippians 3:14 he says, *"I press on towards the goal to win the prize for which God has called me heavenwards in Christ Jesus"* (NIV). Paul was focused on one thing: crossing the finish line. Later, he was able to say, as he neared the end of his life, *"I have finished the race, I have kept the faith"* (2 Timothy 4:7) or as *The Message* puts it: *"This is the only race worth running. I've run hard right to the finish, believed all the way."*

If we keep our attention focused on the finish line, we will not get sidetracked by anything else. I have seen too many people get distracted by relationships, material possessions, achieving status, furthering their career, earning more money, offences or sin; and these things have caused them to lose sight of their goal – the finish line. But it need not be that way!

As you're reading this book, if you are feeling depleted, exhausted and like you are about to give up on the race of life, it may be because you have lost sight of the finish line. I have found that the only times I've ever wanted to give up have been when I've become overwhelmed with my circumstances and lost sight of the bigger picture. Because I lost focus and became consumed with the pressing issues or feelings of the moment, I was tempted to quit. Realising that I am actually in this race to finish it helped get me back on track.

At my fortieth birthday party I remember looking around at all of the wonderful people I have "done life" with. One thing that we all had in common was that we'd each had serious obstacles to overcome and disappointments to process. Some of us had lost loved ones, some had come back from financial ruin; others had had to deal with broken dreams, to fight cancer or struggle with other health issues, to cope with betrayal, to deal with rebellious children. As I reflected on this I realised that the decisive factor that made each one of us "winners" in our individual races was that at every juncture, we chose to see the bigger picture and focus on finishing our race. I lamented for the people I knew should also have been there, but who had dropped out of the race because somewhere along the line they chose to focus on something else, and inevitably ended up dropping out of the race.

Check point 5

The running coach Bill Dellinger said, "Good things come slow – especially in distance running."[4] We have to remember that every mile we run takes us a mile closer to the finish line. Keeping our eyes on the goal will help sustain us for the duration of the race. Our goal is to run our race *and* finish our course.

- A long-distance runner focuses on the goal even though they may still be in the first mile.
- Keep your eyes on the prize like Paul and don't allow other things to distract you.
- The goal is to finish our course.

6. A marathon runner is determined to never give up

At some point in the race, every marathon runner wants to give up. This point is known as "the wall" or the "Red Zone", that critical point eight to ten miles from the finish line when your body is screaming for you to stop and give up. My friend Kylie tells me that although the wall is obviously invisible, it is a very real barrier in the runner's mind. It is the point at which the runner's body is begging for him or her to stop. Their will to go on is almost broken and their mind begins to get hazy. At this critical point, the runner has to press through the wall and make a decision to not give up. It is one thing to determine at the start of the race that you are not going to give up, but quite another in the heat of the race, especially during the exhaustion and pain one experiences when hitting the wall.

I often joke that I think so many God-opportunities have come my way in life just because I'm still here

and others aren't. In other words, God is running short
of options! There are others who started the race with
me who were far more gifted, talented, eloquent,
anointed and smarter than I was, but somewhere along
the line they gave up and I just kept running. There is a
lot to be said for just keeping going even though you
may feel like giving up.

There are two great examples of this from modern-
day Olympic events. They clearly illustrate the
principle that we should never give up, regardless of
what happens to us:

1. In the 2004 Olympics held in Athens, the Brazilian
    marathon runner, Vanderlei de Lima, was leading
    the race. He was running really strongly with only
    three miles to go when suddenly a crazy man
    burst onto the track from the mass of spectators
    and forcibly grabbed de Lima, pulling him into the
    crowd. Security officials eventually got the man
    away and a very shaken de Lima returned to the
    race. By then he'd lost his lead to Italy's Stefano
    Baldini. As he pressed on to the goal he was
    passed by one other runner. De Lima finished third
    and won the bronze medal. The award ceremony
    was an incredible event to witness because never
    before in the history of the Olympics had a third-
    place winner been given such an ovation.
    Everyone knew that de Lima was a winner because
    he had not given up.

2. At the 1968 Olympics, an hour after the marathon winner crossed the finish line, Tanzania's John Stephen Akhwari limped across the finish line having been injured in a fall earlier in the race. When asked why he didn't quit, he said these words (and I think every Christian ought to have similar words imprinted on their spirit): "My country did not send me 7,000 miles to start this race. My country sent me to finish."

Jesus did not put us on this earth just to start the race of life, but to finish it. Paul is a great example of someone who never quit. As he approached the finishing line of his race, towards the end of his life, he wrote these words:

> *"For I am already being poured out as a drink offering, and the time of my departure is at hand. I have fought the good fight, I have finished the race, I have kept the faith."*
>
> (2 Timothy 4:6–7)

Jesus did not put us on this earth just to start the race of life, but to finish it.

My prayer is that these words will be echoed by us as we come to our finish line in life.

Check point 6

Is there any area of your life where you feel you have "hit a wall"? The temptation is always to back off, slow down or quit, but God wants you to press through and carry on. Often, like the Red Zone of marathon running, the "walls" that hinder our progress exist more in our minds than they do in reality. Keeping your eyes fixed on Jesus coupled with a determination to never give up will see you through.

- You may not think you are the most gifted, eloquent, anointed person, but if you are still running, God can use you! God is more interested in your availability than your talent.
- Don't settle for merely starting your race – be determined to finish it.
- Look forward to the day when, like Paul, you can say, "I have finished the race, I have kept the faith."

7. A marathon runner realises that the run is worth the effort

Something which may surprise you, as it did for me when I first discovered it, is the fact that very few marathon runners are paid well for what they do. Only a handful of the world's elite really make a career out of it. The majority are not compensated at all and basically go unheralded. So why on earth would anyone want to put themselves through such an ordeal? Marathon runners run for the immense feeling of accomplishment that it brings and for the buzz of completing the longest race in the world. My friends tell me, "Chris, you have no idea how it feels when I finish the race!" (and she's right, I don't and do not imagine that I ever will). Completing such a demanding course brings an incredibly euphoric, satisfying feeling.

The great thing about running the race of the Christian life is that not only do we receive a similar sense of personal achievement, but that our life has eternal significance. We run for a prize because God has promised to reward our efforts. Paul says, *"Everyone who competes for the prize is temperate in all things. Now they do it to obtain a perishable crown, but we for an imperishable crown"* (1 Corinthians 9:25). In other words, professional athletes compete for a physical medal which in the end will tarnish, but Christians run for an imperishable, eternal reward from God. This makes the run worth the effort.

Back in 2000, Nick and I went to watch the Olympic Games when it was held in Sydney. One of the highlights of the event for me was seeing the multiple world record holding Michael Johnson run his last competitive race before retiring. Johnson, who is known as "The Duck" because of his unorthodox running style, was once asked by a reporter, "If you had a usual running technique like other runners do you think you would go faster?" Johnson responded by saying, "If I ran like all the other runners, I would be back there with them!"

After qualifying for the Summer Olympics, Johnson actually injured himself in the US championships 200 metre final and could not defend his title in that event. But that did not stop him from competing and winning gold in both the 400 metres and the 4×400 metres relay, bringing his total number of Olympic gold medals to five. It was a great end to an illustrious career and to this day, Johnson still holds the world record times in all three of his chosen events.

What really struck me that day, however, was the fact that when it came time to present the medals, it was all over so quickly. After the immense preparation that went into winning the race, the award ceremony was over in a couple of minutes. Johnson stood up, was presented with his medal, they played a bit of the American national anthem, and then they took everything away and the next race started. I remember thinking, "Isn't that astonishing? This man probably hasn't eaten pizza for the last five years! He's gotten up at the crack of dawn for probably the last fifteen years – and all for this fleeting moment of glory, to receive a gold medal (that isn't actually solid gold) for a race that lasted less than a minute!" With that, I just had to go and get another slice of pizza and make myself feel better!

Don't get me wrong, I am not diminishing Johnson's outstanding achievements in any way. His name will be written in the history books and he will be remembered as one of the pre-eminent athletes of his generation. But eventually, his time in the spotlight had to come to and end, and the day will surely come when some young emerging athlete will shatter the records and become the "new" world record holder. All that effort for such momentary gratification, to receive the accolades of man and enjoy the applause of the crowd for a fleeting time. How much more should we be devoted to the cause of running our race? We are not running to win the right to bask in the glory of the crowd for about two minutes; to receive a gold medal (that is actually 92.5% silver in case you were wondering!) and the respect of our peers. We are part of an eternal cause. We are engaged in a mission that changes people's eternal destinies! We are living to receive an accolade from the King of kings – the Creator of the Universe! We are leaving a legacy that is going to considerably outlast us. If people are willing to exercise so much discipline for a race that will last ten seconds, how much more should we run our race with the purpose of winning?

Check point 7

Like most marathon runners, earthly prizes (fame, success or gold medals made out of silver) are not the reason why we run. As Christians, our reward is an eternal inheritance. This is why it's important to remember that our run is worth the effort.

- Earthly prizes are not the goal (Jesus is).
- The crown that we win is eternal.
- When we are motivated by a passion for eternity, our race is worth the effort.

Part 1 Runners Checklist

Before moving on to the next part of the book, *The Art of Running*, reflect again on the following points:

- Remember that life is more like a marathon than a sprint.
- The all important key to running to win is to keep your eyes fixed on Jesus at all times.

There are seven principles that are true for all successful marathon runners that we can apply to our spiritual lives. People who run to win:

- Have a vision for the whole race
- Have a commitment to preparation

- Endure discomfort and pain
- Maintain daily disciplines
- Focus on the goal
- Are determined never to give up
- Realise that the run is worth the effort

Notes

1. Quoted on www.runrepublic.ie
2. Quote from http://en.wikipedia.org/wiki/Juma_Ikangaa
3. Quoted on www.805running.com
4. *Source*: www.twentysix-two.com/running-quotes/

PART 2

Get Set

The art of running

The atmosphere was electric as the eight runners crouched on their starting blocks, coiled like springs, ready to propel themselves forward at the crack of the starting pistol. Close-ups on the massive screen in the stadium flashed a shot of Michael Johnson's face, set like flint, eyes staring straight ahead, focused on one thing and one thing only – crossing that finish line ahead of every other person. After what seemed like an eternity, the shot came and Johnson was gone. Up out of the blocks and away to decimate the competition by a wide margin. Johnson, despite recovering from a recent injury, was unbelievable – a lean, mean running machine.

Poised in his starting blocks and with his eyes fixed on the finish line, I am confident of the fact that Michael Johnson was not thinking, "Gee, I hope I come in the top three!" I'm sure he had long eradicated all thoughts of possible failure. He had come to Australia with a single goal, no plan B. This was, after all, to be the last time he would run in the

Olympics, having announced his retirement, and he wanted to underline his dominance in the 400 metres. He had no other option in mind but to come first and claim the gold.

That day at the Sydney Olympic stadium, there were 116,000 spectators watching, but only eight people who had paid the price necessary to participate in the race. Up until that point, those eight people had spent their lives doing very different things to the rest of us. They had not spent all their time sunbathing on the beach; they had not strolled down to their local coffee shop each morning for a vanilla latte and a Danish! The fact that they had got out of bed at ridiculous hours to train; the fact that they had special diets and a very different lifestyle to most of us played a significant role in enabling them to compete with the world's best (apart from the obvious fact that they were naturally very fast runners). That's why they were in with a chance of winning.

Coupled with the determination to win and a commitment to live a disciplined lifestyle, runners have to be skilled in the art of running. They must have mastered the techniques necessary to compete at a high level. Otherwise, all the determination in the world will not help them. I run regularly to keep fit, but there is a huge difference between running for fitness and running competitively to win a race. Remember that Paul, in 1 Corinthians 9:24–30,

not only exhorts us to run, but to run to win.
The race of life is not a casual jog, but a purpose
driven, intentional race. There is no point
participating in the race of life if you don't intend
to cross the finish line. If we are supposed to be
running to win in life, then it is imperative that we
discover what it is that competitive runners know
about the very act of running that enables them
to do it so much better than others. That's what we
will be exploring throughout this second part of the
book.

When I first started running, frankly, I had no
idea what I was doing. As more seasoned runners
came alongside me and gave me tips, I learnt how to
enjoy my running and thrive in it. Before then, I had
great intentions, but I could only do one lap around
the block and I'd nearly pass out, plus I hated every
second of it! A lot of us are like this with life. After
running with purpose for only a short distance,
we are ready to pass out because we haven't taken
the time to learn to run properly. If we can apply
some sound principles about how to run effectively,
each of us can run in the race of life, love it and
win. Running seems simple enough, but there are
a number of things that can help us to run more
efficiently with greater endurance and at the same
time avoid injury.

A Guide to the Art of Running

1. Runners take a holistic approach to training

The first thing about running is that you cannot separate it from the rest of your life. Running experts say that in order to maximise running performance and minimise the risk of injury, runners should take a "total body" approach. This means that a serious runner has to train their upper body as well as their lower body, their core as much as their limbs, and their brain as much as their heart. To be a strong, healthy runner, you need the whole package: endurance, speed, flexibility, coordination and mental focus. Optimal performance training therefore involves physical preparation, nutrition, mental skills, the right equipment and good technique. You can't just work on one area – all areas are important when you're running to win.

Runners are extremely conscious of what they eat, how long they sleep, what they wear, how long they train for, what they drink, and from whom they are receiving input or coaching. In their lives, everything is interconnected. They don't live a compartmentalised life. They know that they can't train for a few hours and then do what they want for the rest of the week. Every part of their lives affects every other part, so they follow a regular daily routine in the months leading up to a race, and they maintain it afterwards so that they don't lose their edge.

Spiritually speaking, we need a similarly holistic approach to our lives. God created us with a body, a soul and a spirit. We have to ensure that we are looking after each of these aspects of our beings in order to run strong. Rather than a total body approach, we need a "body, soul and spirit" approach. (I talk about developing this "spiritual core" in great detail in my book *Stop Acting Like a Christian ... Just Be One!*)

The apostle Paul spoke this blessing over the Thessalonian Christians:

> *"Now may the God of peace Himself sanctify you completely; and may your whole spirit, soul, and body be preserved blameless at the coming of our Lord Jesus Christ."*
>
> (1 Thessalonians 5:23)

It's interesting that Paul took the trouble to mention every aspect of our beings. It shows us that God is concerned with the whole person, not just the spiritual aspect of our lives. For optimum performance, we need to train ourselves in each of these areas.

God is concerned with the whole person, not just the spiritual aspect of our lives.

Body

Our body is the vehicle that God has given us to take us into our destiny, so common sense tells us that we need to look after it. The often-quoted verse from 1 Corinthians 3:16 reminds us, *"Do you not know that you are the temple of God and that the Spirit of God dwells in you?"* How amazing that God chose the human body as the vessel that would contain His Spirit! What a profound mystery! God obviously thinks that the human body is important or He wouldn't have decided to use it as the dwelling place for His presence. If our bodies are that important to God, they should be important to us too.

There is a wealth of information available today to advise us how best to look after our bodies. It is an issue that we should take seriously because our health is critical to running a great race. We can have the best spiritual intentions but if our body cannot function to its full capacity, we will inadvertently cut short our destiny. We should, to the best of our ability, ensure that we exercise and eat well in order to function well. There is so much knowledge available that we really have no excuse not to be healthy. One has to be reckless or careless to do it!

In 1 Timothy 4:8 Paul writes, *"For bodily exercise profits a little, but godliness is profitable for all things, having promise of the life that now is and of that which is to come."* I have heard so many Christians use this verse as a lame excuse for not looking after their bodies! They say things like, "It's having our heart right with God that counts." That is true. But this verse does not say that exercise doesn't profit one at all! The physical dimension of life cannot be ignored just because "God is more interested in the state of our hearts". In fact, if any group of people have good reason to look after their bodies, it is Christians. We are responsible for outworking the will of God on earth as it is in heaven. We know our bodies are going to wear out and expire eventually, but we don't need them to wear out any quicker than they should! Our aim should be to carry on accomplishing the purposes of God on earth for as long as possible. Christians have more reason to stay fit than any gym junkie. It's not about how good we can make ourselves look by developing lots of muscles, it is about being effective carriers of God and giving Him the best shell possible to work with.

Paul wrote, *"I **discipline** my **body** and bring it into subjection"* (1 Corinthians 9:27, emphasis added). Paul wasn't only spiritually-minded, he was strongly against any abuse of the body, and advised followers of Jesus to avoid sins that could damage their health. This included such things as sexual immorality, gluttony and drunkenness. Paul trained his body to be in submission to his spirit-man. Similarly, each one of us has the ability to exercise self-control through the power of the Holy Spirit working in us. We can "subdue" our bodies and make them do what we want,

just like Paul did. I need to remind myself of this fact
frequently (as I head to the cupboard for another
chocolate bar)!

The sad fact is that some people will simply not fulfil
their destiny because their body cannot take them
there. I'm not trying to put condemnation or guilt upon
anyone because I understand that there are times when
the enemy sends sickness, and our physical health can
be limited in many others ways. But many people are
not helping God out by having a poor diet, lacking any
self-control and by hardly ever exercising. If we
choose to look after our bodies, we will have a greater
chance of running our race and finishing our course.

Nick and I travel over 200,000 air miles each per
year as we go around the world preaching, teaching,
ministering the Word of God and facilitating missions
projects. We wouldn't be able to physically cope with
such a demanding schedule if we weren't fit and
healthy. Even though I know that it is my God-given
destiny to do this, it would be foolish of me to neglect
my physical fitness and then pray, "Oh God, make me
able to do this!" Why should God answer that prayer
if I am not doing my part? Instead, I have to do all that
I can do by exercising properly, taking the correct
nutrition and looking after my body. God will do
what only He can do to supernaturally sustain me
spiritually. We can live beyond asking God for a
healing miracle every week and enjoy living in divine
health by taking care of the shell that He has given us!

Soul

In 3 John 2 the Bible says, *"Beloved, I pray that you may prosper in all things and be in health, just as your soul prospers."* There is no doubt that a healthy soul (meaning our mind, will and emotions) is crucial in order to run to win. Many people with great spiritual gifts and even great health have had their destiny sabotaged simply because they have never learnt to manage their emotions, their wills or their thought lives.

Some Christians make the mistake of thinking that Christianity is all about changing the way we behave (i.e. doing certain things because they are "good" or "righteous" things to be doing, and avoiding other things that are "bad" or "sinful"). But Christianity far transcends external behaviour modification. Christianity is not all about rules and regulations, wearing the right clothes, saying the right things, etc. It is about an internal "heart" transformation. This means that our minds, wills and emotions have to be submitted to the Holy Spirit so that He can begin to change us from the inside out. We can't give our hearts to Christ and then let our emotions or thought lives run out of control.

In the same way that we apply discipline to our bodies, we also need to exercise discipline in the realm of our soul. We have to face the issues that so often dominate our thoughts and feelings and bring them into line with the Word of God (see 2 Corinthians 10:5).

Such issues might include brokenness, unforgiveness, bitterness, rejection, lust, greed, envy, hurt and anger. These are the things that most often sabotage people's destinies. Many people are not using their spiritual gifts to their full potential because they suffer from unresolved issues in their souls. They constantly let themselves down because their emotional issues are never resolved. This soul-weakness is an Achilles heel that will eventually take them out of their race unless they take action to resolve it. We simply *have* to learn to deal with unresolved issues in our past in order to ensure a healthy soul life and therefore a healthy future.

In my book *A Life Unleashed*, I share extensively about the challenges that I faced in my past, which had to be overcome in order for me to step into my God-given destiny. I was left in a hospital unnamed and unwanted when I was born and am living proof that no matter how you start in life, you can overcome the obstacles and hurdles of your past by applying the very principles that I am writing about and run to win. We do not need to live like victims; rather we can appropriate the truth of the Word of God into every area of our lives and experience complete healing and wholeness. If I had never allowed God's Word to bring healing into my life, I would not be fulfilling my destiny now. I might have had the God-given gifts and talents that I needed, but I was so weak emotionally that my soul would not allow me to go where my gifts could take me. It was crucial that I dealt with all the areas of brokenness in my heart.

Our inner world totally affects our outer world. If there is a disparity between what's going on inside our heart and what's happening in our external world, our life will eventually implode; it will break down or blow up. The Bible is full of examples of people who did not run their race and finish their course because they did not deal with issues of their soul.

> **Our inner world totally affects our outer world.**

Saul was such a person. He was a man whose life held much promise but it was never fulfilled. He had a huge amount of potential and talent, but he ended up committing suicide. 1 Samuel 9 says that Saul was the most handsome man in Israel, selected by God to reign over His people when they insisted they needed a king:

> *"And he had a choice and handsome son whose name was Saul. There was not a more handsome person than he among the children of Israel. From his shoulders upward he was taller than any of the people."*

> (1 Samuel 9:2)

God had obviously anointed this young, faithful man who had an obedient heart, a good background and a striking appearance. At first, Saul was humble and conscientious about his task – but pride soon set in. Saul's pride turned to envy and he took matters into his own hands when he saw the possibility of his royal authority being usurped. Saul's brokenness in his soul realm eventually ambushed him. He resented the presence of the talented young David, whom he feared would steal his crown, and became increasingly paranoid and angry. We can see this deficit in his soul revealed when a group of women came singing after David had defeated the Philistines.

> *"So the women sang as they danced, and said:*
>
> > *'Saul has slain his thousands,*
> > *And David his ten thousands.'*
>
> *Then Saul was very angry, and the saying displeased him; and he said, 'They have ascribed to David ten thousands, and to me they have ascribed only thousands. Now what more can he have but the kingdom?' So Saul eyed David from that day forward."*
>
> (1 Samuel 18:7–9)

It was Saul's inability to accept that there were others better than he was that revealed his soul's weakness. He could easily have cheered David on and rejoiced in his exploits – they were, after all, fighting for the same cause. But his longing for power and affirmation turned him bitter and led him to make many wrong decisions. When, like Saul, we continually chase affirmation or are obsessed with being the best, we too are feeding off the wrong stimuli. Saul eventually suffered a total loss of affirmation and was rejected by everyone around him. He fell into depression and despair and then committed suicide.

As we can see from the life of Saul, it is imperative that we deal with the broken, wounded or undeveloped areas in our soul realm if we are going to run to win. We must also realise that it is an ongoing process – one that lasts our whole life. Some people say, "The past is the past. I dealt with that stuff years ago," but I would challenge everyone to consider this: are you so healed that you don't need Jesus any more? There are always areas that God wants to work on in our lives. Admitting that we need help doesn't imply a lack of faith. Some say, "By faith I am whole." I would agree and say the same thing, but I also know that there is a process that I must go through in order to walk out the fullness of the healing that Jesus died to give me. The key is a constant and ongoing submission to the Holy Spirit as He ministers into our lives.

Spirit

If we are going to run to win, we also need to continually feed our spirit. This is the eternal part of our being that is awakened once we are born again. After being "reborn" when we come to Christ, we begin a process whereby we grow, develop and strengthen spiritually. The Bible records that John the Baptist, "... *grew and became strong in spirit, and was in the deserts till the day of his manifestation to Israel"* (Luke 1:80).

How do we become "strong in spirit"? There are numerous ways: these include absorbing God's Word, prayer, fasting, reading books, being planted in a life-giving local church, listening to biblical teaching CDs and being a worshipper. We often neglect doing these things because we become too caught up with the frantic pace of everyday life and have little time to give to spiritual concerns. We focus on the finite, temporal aspect of life and lose sight of the infinite, eternal, spiritual aspect. We need to learn to silence the distractions and voices that daily bombard us in order to make time and space to build our spiritual man. I love the verse in Romans which says,

> *"For those who live according to the flesh set their minds on the things of the flesh, but those who live according to the Spirit, the things of the Spirit. For to be carnally minded is death, but to be spiritually minded is life and peace."*
>
> (Romans 8:5–6)

If we want to be sure of running a great race, we need to feed our spirit and observe the simple disciplines that will ensure that we have a high level of spiritual health and wellbeing. We must always remember that although our body and soul are important without a doubt, it is only our spirit that is eternal. We must therefore always prioritize the strengthening of our spirit man.

Christians cannot afford to live compartmentalised lives. We have one life and that is the life we have in Christ. That is why it is so important to take care of our body, soul and spirit and take a holistic approach to

> **We have one life and that is the life we have in Christ.**

running our race. If we neglect one area, we compromise our race fitness; but if we take a "whole person" approach and realise that every area of our life is interconnected, we begin to run the race of life in a whole, integrated way that is pleasing to God.

Check point 1

Every aspect of our lives is interconnected, so we must take a holistic approach to training and disciplining ourselves. Our bodies, souls and spirits are all important and each of these aspects of our beings needs care and nurture.

- God cares about our bodies – He made them to carry His presence. What changes do you need to make to maintain a healthy diet and exercise?
- Decide to deal with any soul issues that you may have, such as unresolved hurt from the past or persistent negative emotions such as pride, jealousy or anger. Don't let "soul weakness" hinder your race.
- Maintain a discipline of feeding your spirit by reading God's Word, praying, worshipping and meeting with other believers. Add to that other activities that will build you up such as listening to preaching CDs.

2. Runners build a strong foundation

Marathon runners aim to create a strong foundation for themselves by doing lots of long-distance running and endurance training. They don't simply do "more running" – over time, they construct an aerobic foundation and plumbing system that will enable them to run great distances when required. They increase their cardiovascular and lung capacity so that their body can respond to the demands made on it when running a marathon. They also do lots of resistance training to develop their strength and to prevent injury.

Training to be a great runner involves a lot of boring, repetitive, hard work that often seems far removed from the reality of the race. But if runners don't do this "ground work" they won't have the necessary foundation to run to win. In the same way, we often think that God is taking a really long time to bring about the destiny we were born for, not realising that He is busy doing the necessary ground work in us. If we can't see anything obvious happening externally, we have a tendency to think what we are presently doing is a waste of time. To us, it seems far removed from what we know God has called us to do in the future.

The reality is that no experience is wasted in God's economy. Those seemingly insignificant things that we are doing now are *the very things* that are preparing, training and shaping us for what we will be doing for God in the future (that is assuming, of course, that we are on track with the purposes of God). Our present circumstances are a fertile training ground for future success. God is busy building a strong foundation in us that will support us in the future. He is building strength and endurance into us so that we won't waver when demands are placed upon us.

I think back to my days as a youth leader. Driving kids to youth group each week and constantly travelling around speaking to very small groups of people could have been considered pretty mundane and a far cry from what I was ultimately called to do. But I realise now that God was using that experience to build in me a tenacity and "stickability" that enables me to do what I do today. I now travel and speak at different events around the world almost every week of my life. If God hadn't trained me to do this by beginning small and gradually laying a firm foundation, there is no way that I could cope with what I am doing now.

> **No experience is wasted in God's economy.**

Years of driving out to country towns in New South Wales (my home state) and speaking to groups of people, training leaders, winning the lost and implementing social justice projects laid a foundation in my life that now enables me to conduct global missions. There were plenty of times when it seemed tedious – I had a heart to reach nations and instead I was called upon to drive twenty minutes up the road and speak to a few dozen people. Nevertheless, God used that experience to develop in me patience, strength and endurance.

Zechariah 4:10 cautions us, *"Do not despise the day of small beginnings, for the LORD rejoices to see the work begin"* (NLT). If King David had not spent untold hours looking after sheep, he would never have been able to kill a lion and a bear. If he had not had to contend with lions and bears, he would not have had the courage to tackle Goliath. And if David had never faced Goliath, he would have probably remained in obscurity. There was a clear development from one stage of his life to the next. Too many people want to short-cut their foundational training programme but you can't expect to go the distance without having a strong foundation.

Check point 2

We have to cooperate with God's programme of groundwork in our lives if we are to have the right foundation for future success. Focusing on strengthening our spiritual foundations now will increase our capacity to run to win in the future as God presents us with bigger challenges.

- Do not despise the seemingly insignificant things that we are doing now as they are the very things that are preparing, training and shaping us for what we will be doing for God in the future.
- Remember that if we are faithful in the small things that God has given us to do now, He will be able to trust us with bigger things in the future.
- Don't try to short-cut God's training programme for your life – If you want to take out a giant, you must first master the bear.

3. Runners start slowly and build gradually

In order to improve the body's ability to sustain high-intensity effort for long periods of time, runners have to increase their exercise volume by training longer, working harder and increasing speed. But they do this *gradually*, over time. If they overdo an increase in mileage, intensity or speed too soon, they will burn out or get injured. Many runners starting out make the mistake of running too fast, too far, too soon. In reality, you can't run flat out or for a very long time every single day. You have to train for endurance first and for speed later.

> **The race of the Christian life is not a competition.**

Our Christian life is all about running our race so that we last the whole distance. This is why God cares so much about endurance. He is not as concerned about how quickly we reach our destiny as much as He is concerned that we endure and complete our course. The race of the Christian life is not a competition – we don't need to try to keep up with anyone else. We just have to run *our* race and finish *our* course. We must stay focused on that which God has called us to do and remember that God builds gradually. Isaiah tell us,

"For precept must be upon precept, precept upon precept, line upon line, line upon line, here a little, there a little" (Isaiah 28:10).

The principle of building "line by line" can be applied to every area of our life. It is the way in which we build strong marriages, great families, great friendships, healthy bodies, prosperous businesses and fruitful ministries. In other words, it is consistency and commitment that wins races. As an old Indian proverb states, "You walk a mile one step at a time." It is important that we start slowly and build gradually.

In the book of 2 Samuel chapter 18 we read the fascinating story of Ahimaaz – a young man who ran before he was ready. The story gives us insight into the importance of preparation, but also timing. The background to the story is that Absalom, King David's own son, had been trying to usurp him as king. On the day recounted in chapter 18, Absalom had been defeated in battle by David's army and killed. Ahimaaz approached Joab, the commander of David's army, and begged to be the one who would deliver news of the victory to David himself. Joab was not willing to let him do it and said, *"You shall not take the news this day, for you shall take the news another day. But today you shall take no news, because the king's son is dead"* (2 Samuel 18:20).

Joab was obviously sensitive to the fact that Absalom, despite trying to usurp David, was still his son. He knew that David would be deeply grieved by the news of his death. Ahimaaz clearly hadn't thought this through. He was young and naïve. In essence, Joab was telling Ahimaaz, "Look, you're not ready to run right now. You're going to have another day, but this isn't your day. You are not ready to take such momentous news to the king." With that, Joab turned around and commissioned another man, a Cushite, to run and tell the king what had happened. However, Ahimaaz didn't take his commander's advice and persisted and persisted. *"Whatever happens, please let me also run after the Cushite,"* he says in verse 22. Joab replies to him saying, *"Why will you run, my son, since you have no news ready?"* In other words, "You ain't going nowhere, because you've got nothing to say!"

Ahimaaz, however, kept at it and eventually was allowed to run. The Bible says that he ran after the Cushite, who should have taken the news of Absalom's death, and outran him. Ahimaaz took a shortcut and arrived in the king's presence before the Cushite. It is obvious from the verses that follow that Ahimaaz was totally out of his depth. He wasn't ready for such a task and you can see him stammering a feeble response to king David's query, *"Is the young man Absalom safe?"* (verse 29). He actually fudges an answer by saying, *"I saw a great tumult, but I did not know what it was about"* (verse 29). He knew very well that Absalom was dead! David's response was swift: *"Turn aside and stand here"* (verse 30). One of David's men had spotted the Cushite approaching and it was he who finally delivered the piece of information that David actually wanted. I'm not sure that there is anything worse than realising that not only are you in a place that you absolutely should not be in, but also that you don't have the capacity, resources, talent, or information that you need to carry out what needs to be done in the situation.

No matter what you do, you cannot run ahead of God's timing. If you do, you are in danger of being swept aside and overwhelmed by the discovery that you are not up to the task at hand. We always want to reach our destination sooner rather than later, but God will have His way and the person who is meant to be fulfilling a certain task at a certain time will be there! We have to learn to run our race in the time that God has ordained.

God has set a pace for my race.

One of the major lessons that I have learnt in life is that everything always takes longer than I thought it would. Every big promotion in my life has come "suddenly", but each "suddenly" was usually preceded by ten years. There have always been more challenges than I anticipated, but in the end, God's will and promises prevail. My personality type is such that I want everything to happen "yesterday" and nothing ever moves quickly enough for me. But no matter how hard I have pushed, I have discovered that God has set a pace for my race. If we can all just learn to accept that, our lives will be full of much more joy and peace!

Check point 3

Keep in mind the following principles:

- God is more concerned about building endurance in you than He is about getting you to your destination quickly.
- Remember to stay focused on what it is that you are meant to be doing and don't rush ahead of God – build gradually and don't run before you are ready like Ahimaaz!

---

4. Runners need the right fuel

What runners eat and drink is crucial. They need lots of protein for muscle repair and lots of calcium to protect their bones from fractures. Caffeine and alcohol can lead to dehydration, so they minimise these. Runners have to eat a full breakfast well in advance of a race so that they don't get stomach cramps or nausea whilst running. In short, runners constantly need to be careful to fuel their bodies properly so they don't run out of steam. They need the right mix of carbohydrates, protein and healthy fats as well as constant hydration.

Spiritually speaking, it is exactly the same for us. If we are going to run to win, we have to learn to feast on the right things and avoid those things that will detract from our race fitness. The most basic ingredient needed in our diet is the Word of God. The Bible says in Joshua 1:8,

> *"This Book of the Law shall not depart from your mouth, but you shall meditate in it day and night, that you may observe to do according to all that is written in it. For then you will make your way prosperous, and then you will have good success."*

The fuel of God's Word taken daily strengthens us to run our race. We also need to feed ourselves by being constantly saturated in God's presence. One way of doing this is to spend time just waiting on God, spending time in His presence, listening to His voice and doing what He tells us to do. Isaiah 40:31 promises that,

> *"Those who wait on the LORD*
> *Shall renew their strength;*
> *They shall mount up with wings like eagles,*
> *They shall run and not be weary,*
> *They shall walk and not faint."*

If we are going to run a great race and not grow weary or faint, we have to learn to wait on God. Some people think this means sitting in a room meditating, just waiting, waiting and waiting, and forty years later they're still waiting for God! I think this scripture speaks more about "waiting" in the sense of a waiter waiting on a table. This is an active and not a passive thing. We need to be waiting on God and asking Him, "What's your order Lord? What's your will? What's your purpose for me?"

People often ask me how I manage to keep going at such a pace all the time. I believe that it's because I am constantly waiting on God (at least I try to), seeking to hear what He wants me to do next and carrying out His plan for my life. Waiting on God sustains me. When you are executing God's will in His strength, it is a lot easier than struggling and striving to achieve something yourself. If we cooperate with Him, God will grace us to do what we need to do in order to run our course and finish our race.

Another ingredient in maintaining a healthy spiritual diet is to ensure we are constantly being filled with the Holy Spirit. Ephesians 5:18 says, *"And do not be drunk with wine, in which is dissipation; but be filled with the Spirit."* And again in Acts 1:8, *"You shall receive power when the Holy Spirit has come upon you."* The sustenance to run our race must come from the empowerment of the Holy Spirit. In fact, Paul says that we can experience being filled with the Spirit on a *daily basis*. It is not a one-off experience, but an ongoing process.

We also need to saturate ourselves in praise and worship. Psalm 22:26 says, *"Those who seek the LORD will praise him"* (NIV). Praise and worship are like water to our soul and spirit. When I look back and think about how I managed to live through the darkest hours in my life, I realise the thing that kept me going was the song of the Lord. I got through by focusing on praising and worshipping God. The Psalmist also wrote, *"Praise be to the LORD, for he showed his wonderful love to me when I was in a besieged city"* (Psalm 31:21 NIV). Worshipping God will actually sustain and protect you as He envelopes you in His presence.

God is our manufacturer and He knows how we work best. We need the kind of premium unleaded, supercharged fuel that I have just discussed. This is the spiritual diet that will enable us to run to win. We cannot live on a diet of ungodly, immoral, negative input and then expect to run well. It's simply not going to happen. We've got to put the things of God into our beings if we are going to get out the life God has called us to live.

Check point 4

Meditating on God's Word, spending time in His presence, being filled with the Spirit, praise and worship, and prayer and fasting are the dietary ingredients that build winning runners in the race of life. Remember these two important facts:

- "Feasting" on the things that you know will build you up and avoiding those things that will damage you will dramatically increase your race fitness.
- What we put into our lives will determine what comes out of them. Quality input will result in quality output.

---

5. Runners eradicate dead weight

All serious runners wear clothing designed to help them function at their best. When I went to the 2000 Olympics, I didn't see any of the finalists in the track events wearing mountain climbing gear! None of them decided to compete in ski suits either! Instead, each of them had shed all unnecessary layers of clothing and they ran in light, breathable, skin-tight gear, purpose-made for running. In the same way, we need to be properly clothed for running our spiritual race. We can do this by following the advice of Hebrews 12:1 that instructs us to *"throw off everything that hinders ... "* (NIV). We don't want to carry any excess weight – we need to be streamlined for maximum efficiency.

Most running injuries are said to occur because of people wearing the wrong type of footwear. I heard a story about a well-known TV celebrity in London who turned up to run a marathon race wearing bowling shoes. Despite being told by a fellow runner that her inappropriate footwear would cause her problems, she went ahead regardless. She was forced to drop out of the race after less than ten miles in agony with numerous blisters. You have to wear the right gear if you are going to compete and last the distance.

The NKJV Bible puts Hebrews 12:1 this way:

> *"Therefore we also, since we are surrounded by so great a cloud of witnesses, let us lay aside every weight, and the sin which so easily ensnares us, and let us run with endurance the race that is set before us."*

The fact that the writer to the Hebrews tells us to lay aside *"every weight"* and *"the sin which so easily ensnares"* suggests to me that there is a difference between a "weight" and a "sin". In other words, if you are not running to your optimum capacity, it may not be because of some gross sin you are committing, but because of an unnecessary "weight" that is holding you back. For example: a "weight" in this context could be the fact that you consistently hang out with the wrong people. They may or may not be Christians, but for whatever reason, they are holding you back from aspiring to greater things in Christ. Perhaps they are feeding you with negativity and dragging you down to their level instead of encouraging and building you up. It may sound a little harsh but you need to shed some of that weight!

You have to minimise everything that is holding you back so you can move forward and allow God to propel you into the future He has prepared for you.

Maybe your "weight" is the fact that you have reached a plateau in your Christian life and don't know how to break through to the next level. For instance, you may be looking to God for a financial breakthrough. It could be that God is challenging you to actually give more and be stretched in your faith, and therein lies the key to your breakthrough. If you know that God has spoken to you about this but you are holding back from doing it, this is a weight that is preventing you from progressing. It's not a sin, but it is a weight!

We need to continually look at our lives and see where we can shed weight, casting off any excess layers that are adding nothing to our racing gear and slowing us down. We need to keep ourselves streamlined and flexible in order to what God calls us to do.

The writer to the Hebrews does tell us to lay aside every sin, as well as every weight. It is very possible for us to have sin in our lives that is damaging our race fitness. If your heart has unforgiveness or bitterness in it, hurt or rejection, lust or greed, you are not a fit runner! Perhaps you are compromising in areas of your life – looking at inappropriate Internet sites or magazines which are destroying your intimacy with God and your relationships with others. Sin must be dealt with ruthlessly and cast aside. God won't do that for us: *we* need to lay aside our sin and repent of it. Once we shed those sins and weights, we will no longer stumble along but run freely. Make a decision today to take off those excess layers that are holding you back and start running effectively.

In order to keep stepping up to new levels in my life, I have had to consistently choose to "lay aside" the weight of unsaved family members who tried to give me ungodly counsel. Similarly, the weight of Christian friends who no longer had the desire to keeping pressing deeper into the presence of God, choosing comfort, complacency and mediocrity instead. I had to lay aside the weight of my Greek Orthodox culture and religious traditions in order to keep running my race. On top of that, I must continually lay aside the weight of my own limited and contained thinking, replacing it with God's thoughts, and I must deal with the sins of offence, unforgiveness and jealousy in my own heart so that I can continue to run my race unhindered. It is a daily decision to choose to lay aside those things that hold us back from running our race and finishing our course.

Check point 5

Just as professional runners will make themselves as streamlined as possible for maximum efficiency when running, we need to get rid of any "excess baggage" that is stopping us from running to our full capacity. Things that hold us back can be defined as either "weights" or "sins". Take time out to review your life and be honest with yourself about the things that are holding you back. Make a decision to take these things to God in prayer and ask for His help in dealing with them.

- Take the writer of Hebrews' advice and "throw off" anything that is holding you back from running your race. Don't try to run with excess baggage.
- List those things you need to deal with and distinguish between sins that need to be repented of and weights that you need to lay aside.

6. Runners have rest days

For runners, rest and sleep are not luxuries, they are necessities. Sleep plays a vital role in restoring the body because intense running produces inflammation and micro-tears in the muscles. One complete day of rest every week is essential as part of a runner's weekly training schedule. Training day in and day out without a break leaves runners feeling very stale, weary and unmotivated because the body needs recreation time.

"Recreation" is an interesting word. It means precisely what it says: we need time to allow our self-regenerating body to be "re-created". Rest and recreation have been part of God's plan for man from the very beginning. He even modelled it for us Himself by working on creation for six days and then taking a day off.

> **Rest and recreation have been part of God's plan for man from the very beginning.**

As global communications technology continues to advance, a significant trade-off is that our lives get busier and busier. We can communicate with others at any time in any place in the world with amazing speed and clarity, but this has resulted in increased pressure and stress as people are pushed to achieve more and do it quickly! We have to ensure that we don't get caught up in all this frantic activity for the wrong reasons and end up sacrificing our families, our values, our morality and our health just to attain false goals of "success".

Exodus 20:9 begins with the word, *"Remember"*. This is God's way of saying, "You are likely to forget in the busyness of life, so *remember* you were designed to need a day of rest." We are created in the image of God, so if God needed a rest day after six days of working hard, how much more do we? The instant nature of our society – our food, our entertainment, our communication and our travel – can have such a great effect on our lives that we never slow down enough to recover. But spending time with family and friends and taking a break from the pressures of life is exactly what we need to recuperate and restore our energy levels.

Nick and I are very aware that we lead unbelievably full lives. It is not unusual for us to be in six different countries in the space of one month. We travel with our two young children and have an office in Sydney where we lead a great staff and team. We are constantly teaching, preaching, writing books and dealing with all the issues of running an international ministry. But we have learnt that in the midst of all of the pressures and demands on our lives and time, we cannot afford *not* to take time out to rest and recuperate. In order to stay fresh, creative and hearing from God, we need to make time in our lives to simply "do nothing". We are always reminding each other that we need to enjoy the journey, and that if we are going to actually last the distance, we need to take time to rest. To help that process, we schedule times of recreation during our week and ensure that we have fantastic family vacations. In my early years of ministry, I rarely if ever took the time to rest and recreate, and the resulting physical and emotional toll on my life almost took me out of the race. I have learnt the hard way that if I am going to cross the finish line, I must make time to rest!

Check point 6

Rest is not just a good idea but God's idea. He showed us the importance of it by modelling it for us Himself. Rest is part of God's plan for our lives and if we cooperate with it, we will find that we run with a greater efficiency and purpose. God's desire for us is not that we merely "rest from work", but that we "work from a place of rest", abiding in Him and allowing Him to recharge our spiritual batteries.

Ask yourself the following question and take any appropriate action to respond:

- Do I allow the pressures of modern-day living to drive me, or is a regular time of rest a priority for me?

Part 2 Runners Checklist

Before moving on to the final part of the book, think about the important lessons we have learned:

- Along with the determination to win and a commitment to live a different lifestyle, runners have to be skilled in the art of running.

There are six aspects involved in the art of running that we can learn from and apply to our spiritual lives. People who run to win:

- Take an holistic approach
- Build a strong foundation
- Start slowly and build gradually
- Maintain a healthy diet
- Eradicate dead weight
- Have rest days

In the ideal world, every individual would be running strongly in their lane and completing the course set out for him or her by God, but it is clear that not everyone is doing that. Some still struggle to make progress because their paths are blocked by obstacles that have the potential to take them out of the race. In the final section of this book we will be looking at the most common obstacles we face that can threaten to disqualify us and how to deal with them.

PART 3

Go!

Finishing strong

The Olympic Games has had more than its fair share of scandal over the years due to the number of athletes who have been disqualified from competition. Today, most disqualifications occur because of the illegal use of performance-enhancing drugs (in other words, cheating!) But there have been numerous other causes:

- Back in 1912, a US decathlete was stripped of his gold medal after it was discovered that he had played professional baseball for one summer, three years earlier, thus negating his "amateur" status.
- In 1932, a silver medallist in an equestrian event was demoted to last place for breaking the rules by making "clicking" noises to urge his horse on. He maintained his story (to no avail) that it was his "creaking saddle" that was making the noises!
- In the 1968 Winter Olympics, three German competitors in the women's luge event (a luge is a one- or two-person sled) were disqualified because they had been illegally "heating up" their sled's runners before their race!

The list could go on and on. It might surprise you to hear that I have been disqualified myself when competing in sporting events in the past. I was disqualified from the under sixteens' 400 metres track final because I false started twice (even though I am certain to this day that I didn't move before the gun!). I was also disqualified from the 200 metre final because it was decreed by the race marshal that my foot strayed into the adjacent lane. I could have sworn that I didn't and that the red marks on my white running shoes were a figment of his imagination!

As funny as this sounds now, no one likes being disqualified. It can be a humiliating experience. More importantly, no one wants to be disqualified from the race of life – yet we all have the potential to be disqualified. No matter how well we run or how competent we are, there is always the possibility that we will do something to put ourselves out of the race. Regardless of what stage of our race we are at, there will always be challenges and obstacles that, if not dealt with correctly, will cause us to trip.

The apostle Paul, who did so much to build the early Church and reach the lost, never assumed he would automatically make it to the finish line of his race and was careful not to be presumptuous. In 1 Corinthians 9:27 he says, *"I discipline my body and make it my slave, so that, after I have preached to others, I myself **will not be disqualified**"* (NASB, emphasis added).

Paul recognised that despite all he had accomplished for the cause of Christ he still had the potential to be disqualified. And if Paul knew that, how much more should we? Therefore, we must be aware of the things that can block our progress and disqualify us from the race.

A Guide to Finishing Strong

Over the years, there have been certain principles that I have learnt that have been pivotal in helping me to keep running strong and avoid disqualification. Most of these principles are simple yet profound: they are spiritual common sense, but incredibly effective if applied consistently to our lives. I encourage you to work through the principles in this guide and apply them to your own life. You will soon find that these will help keep you on track.

1.Winners obey God's rules

In order to compete in and win an Olympic running event, there are certain basic rules that the runners must adhere to. If they fail to comply with the rules as laid down by the sport's governing body, they will be disqualified – it's as simple as that. Some of the most famous runners on the planet have fallen foul of competition rules and have been disqualified as a result. This tells me that no matter who you are (even if you are the very best in your field), you have to abide by the rules or you are out! How sad when an athlete puts so much time and effort into training and makes such great sacrifices for their sport ... and then gets himself or herself disqualified by breaking the rules. What a waste!

The rules that Olympic runners have to abide by (paraphrased in my own words) are as follows:

1. Runners are disqualified after two false starts.
2. Runners in a sprint must remain in their lane throughout the race. If they go into someone else's lane, even accidentally, they are disqualified.
3. Runners must start behind the line. No one is allowed to start a race even a fraction of an inch in front of the line.
4. Runners must wear appropriate athletic shoes and clothing. It doesn't matter if a runner feels more comfortable running without any shoes, the rules say that all runners must wear appropriate gear. Anyone who refuses cannot compete.
5. Runners are disqualified if they impede another runner's progress by obstructing, jostling or interfering.

These rules are not intended to limit the athletes who are taking part; they are designed to maximise every individual's potential to win. The Olympic Committee are not trying to make it more difficult for runners to compete. On the contrary, they want each person to have an equal opportunity to run their race unhindered and finish their course.

In the same way, God has created certain rules for us to live by which are found in His Word. These rules are not intended to contain us, but to maximise our potential. God is our manufacturer and therefore knows best how we work. If we abide by the instructions in God's Word, we will position ourselves to win in life.

The clearest set of "rules for the race" in the Bible is the Ten Commandments. Notice that the Bible doesn't call them the Ten Suggestions! A lot of people live their lives as if God has given us broad guidelines that really aren't that important. God in fact *commands us* to live according to these rules because He knows that they will help us and our society to function at the highest possible level. The motive behind these rules is love, designed to enable us to run to win. Some people accuse the Bible of being archaic, outdated and irrelevant (mostly people who have never read it)! Nothing could be further from the truth. The Bible is living, vital and relevant. God knows how to maximise our potential and His guidebook shows us how to live our lives passionately and with purpose. Society has created hundreds of thousands of laws and bylaws, rules and regulations, but no one has ever been able to improve on the Ten Commandments (refresh your memory be re-reading them in Exodus chapter 20).

Winning in life is a natural by-product of obedience to God's law. Conversely, failure or disqualification can be a by-product of disobedience. If we break God's rules, there are consequences. Disobeying God's rules is like deciding to drive on the wrong side of the road late at night. We have the power and choice to do it, but we are likely to end up killing ourselves and someone else as a consequence. Like any good parent, the boundaries that God establishes for us are there for our protection. When God says that we shouldn't be sleeping around, committing adultery or fornicating, it is because He knows that such activities lead to sexual diseases, broken hearts, damaged emotions and wounded souls. When God tells us not to covet things that belong to other people, it is because He knows that we will never be truly happy until we are content with what He has already blessed us with.

There are plenty of people who pay lip service to living God's way, but aren't really prepared to obey His Word when it comes to the crunch. Those who want to run to win make every effort to align themselves with the Word of God because the Bible says, *"To obey is better than sacrifice"* (1 Samuel 15:22 NIV), and *"Be doers of the word, and not hearers only, deceiving yourselves"* (James 1:22).

Many Christians are not running to win because they are hearing the Word but not doing it! We will never reach our full potential whilst there is a disparity between what we know and what we put into practice. If you want to live a passionate, purpose-driven, victorious, overcoming Christian life, you've got to do what God says. You can't have the results you want without obeying the rules.

Check point 1

No matter how gifted or anointed we are, we cannot disobey God's fundamental rules for living and expect to run to win. If we want to live life passionately and with purpose, we need to familiarise ourselves with the rules!

- God's rules are not intended to contain us, but rather to release us to fulfil our potential.
- Winning in life is a natural by-product of obeying God's law (i.e. His Word).

---

2. Winners fix their eyes on Jesus

The Bible says in Hebrews 12:1–2,

> *"Therefore we also, since we are surrounded by so great a cloud of witnesses, let us lay aside every weight, and the sin which so easily ensnares us, and let us run with endurance the race that is set before us, **looking unto Jesus**, the author and finisher of our faith."*
>
> (emphasis added)

We know that each runner must remain in their designated lane in a track race. This prevents runners from impeding each other and helps them keep a clear view of the path ahead and the finish line. In spiritual terms, we also need to stay focused and not allow ourselves to be distracted by what others are doing. Looking around while we are running instead of focusing on the goal will easily get us off track. The writer of Hebrews gives us the solution: if we keep our eyes fixed on Jesus then we won't veer off course in life.

I recently heard a radio interview with a lady who is now an experienced marathon runner with many races under her belt. She recalled running her first ever marathon, which she described as "disastrous" for one very simple reason: she didn't have the finish line "in the right place". She had thought mistakenly that she had to run 26 miles, when in fact the distance is 26.2 miles. When she reached the 25.6 mile marker she said to herself, "OK, now I can sprint to the finish line." When she reached the 26-mile marker, however, to her horror there was no finish line and she had already given her all. She said that by the time she reached the *real* finish line, she felt like dying because she had sprinted way too early. She thought that she had her race under control, but she was actually focusing on the wrong thing!

Many people begin their race with their eyes fixed on Jesus but get distracted and end up focusing on numerous other things: people, possessions, position, status, gifts, their spouses, their career. They mistakenly think that these things will complete them as a person and help them to achieve their destiny. But the apostle Paul makes it clear in Philippians 1:6 that only Jesus can and will do this for us:

> *"Being confident of this very thing, that **He who has begun a good work in you will complete it** until the day of Jesus Christ."*
>
> (emphasis added)

The source of our completion is found nowhere else but in Christ. Nothing else in life can totally fulfil us – not our marriage partner, children, any amount of material possessions, accolades or achievements – as important to life as they may be. God loves to bless our lives and so He gives us many precious gifts in the

The source of our completion is found nowhere else but in Christ.

form of people and material blessings, but these are not the goal of our lives in and of themselves. Our goal is to complete the course set out for us by God and to become more and more like Jesus along the way. Jesus is both the beginning and the end of our race. If today you are feeling emptied out, distracted and exhausted, it may be because you have lost sight of the source of your completion. If so, it's time to refocus and fix your eyes on Jesus again.

Check point 2

Ask yourself the following questions and then talk to God about what action you need to take if necessary:

- Have I become distracted by the concerns of life and lost sight of the source of my completion?
- What action do I need to take in order to refocus my attention on Jesus and get back in the race?

---

3. Winners learn to love self-control

Self-control is not something we hear a lot about in our twenty-first-century society. We have become increasingly liberal as a society and have made every effort to cast off all restraint in the name of "freedom of choice" and the "rights of the individual". Yet the Bible insists that self-control is both the hallmark of a real Christian and a natural by-product of living righteously for God.

Self-control is mentioned as one of the "fruits of the Spirit" in the most famous passage of Paul's letter to the Galatians (Galatians 5:22–23). Paul says that these are the things that characterise the life of a person who is on track with God:

- Love
- Joy
- Peace
- Kindness
- Goodness
- Faithfulness
- Gentleness
- *Self-control*

The list is meant to be a contrast to what Paul has mentioned in the previous verses: the attributes of a life that is not surrendered to God: sexual immorality, impurity, jealousy, selfishness and many more. What characterises this list of negative characteristics more than anything else is a *lack of self-control.* Without this vital spiritual resource, people are liable to do whatever they like whenever they feel like it. Without self-control, we are easily led astray by our emotions and our own selfish desires. When this happens, we tend to get off track with our God-given destiny and are no longer running to win.

I was talking to a neighbour a little while ago who told me that her husband had walked out on her and left her to look after their two children alone, one aged five and the other seven. On one occasion, she spoke to him on the phone and demanded, "How can you do this to our kids? Even if your feelings towards me have dried up, what about our kids?" Surprised, he responded, "No one else has ever asked me that. Everyone says, 'What about you? How do you feel? You need to be true to your feelings and do what you want to do. Therefore, I haven't really thought about how this would affect them.'"

We are immersed in a culture that thrives on pleasing "self", but we need to go against the flow and set Christ as our goal not self-fulfilment. When we do this, the fruit of His Spirit will be evident in us and we will not sabotage our destiny by making bad decisions. Society's answer is always "do what feels right for you; go with your feelings; do what your heart is telling you to do..." But this is often an excuse that enables us to abdicate our personal responsibility for our actions and the consequences that they have for others. If we want to find God's best for our lives and truly maximise our potential, we need to live a different way. We need to learn to love self-control.

Check point 3

Are there areas in your life where you lack self-control and are not seeing that fruit of the Spirit manifest in your life? Remember that it is a consistent commitment to doing the "basics" of the Christian life, combined with a constant "re-filling" of the Holy Spirit, that will produce the right fruit in your life. Remember to:

- Read the Bible
- Pray
- Wait on God
- Spend time in praise and worship
- Ask God to fill you afresh with the Holy Spirit regularly

4. Winners stay passionate

Passion will consistently energise us and help us to run the full course of our race. People do what they *want to do* in life as a result of passion, but they do what they *have to do* out of obligation. We must never allow our Christian lives to become a boring obligation or a religious ritual instead of a passionate love affair with Jesus Christ. People usually get tired of long-term obligations and when they do, they generally give them up or look for a way out.

There is an "inner drive" that causes runners to pay the huge cost and make the sacrifices that are required in order to reach an Olympic final. They do it because they have one desire and that desire overrides all other concerns, which are seen only as peripheral. No one forces them to behave this way – they do it because they have a passion. One story that illustrates this principle so clearly is the extraordinary tale of Felix Carvajal, a Cuban runner who competed in the marathon event of the 1904 St Louis Olympics.

In the early 1900s, it was common for athletes to be un-sponsored, under-funded amateurs. This was true of

Felix, a postal worker from Havana. He couldn't get any government sponsorship so he quit his job and ran repeatedly around the town square until he had raised enough money in the form of donations from individuals to get the money needed for his passage to New Orleans.

Unfortunately, upon arrival in the United States, he was lured into a crooked game of street dice and lost all his remaining funds – the money that was supposed to pay for his journey from New Orleans to St Louis. It was a disaster, but although he had been foolish, he refused to give up on his dream of running the marathon. So passionate was he about competing that he walked/hitchhiked the 700 miles from New Orleans to St Louis! Upon his arrival, the American weight lifting team took pity on him and provided him with food and shelter. On the day of the marathon, Felix turned up to compete in a pair of trousers, a long-sleeved shirt and what amounted to a pair of dress shoes. A passing discus thrower who happened to have a pair of scissors offered to cut the legs and arms off his clothes for him. It was, after all 90°F and summer in St Louis!

Felix took the field with thirty-nine other runners. The sweltering weather conditions and the fact that race officials had only provided one water station twelve miles into the race meant that many had to retire from heat exhaustion or injury (mainly stomach cramps). One runner, Len Tau, was chased a mile off course through a cornfield by an angry dog!

Despite his complete lack of training and the absence of correct running gear, Felix managed to come fourth in the marathon, just missing out on a medal. Commentators of the race suggested that he could have won the race were it not for these mitigating factors. One thing Felix could not be accused of, however, is lacking passion. He was determined to compete and he was determined to finish his race, despite the odds stacked against him.

> **We will run to win when we live life from the "inside out".**

Despite being thwarted at every juncture, Felix pursued his goal until he achieved it. He could have given up right at the beginning when he couldn't get any sponsorship, or in New Orleans when he lost all his money. He could have said, "It's pointless trying, I don't have the correct clothing." But, however bleak the outlook, he wasn't going to just lie down and give up! He was far too passionate for that!

Similarly, we will run to win when we live life from the "inside out" – fuelled by a passion that comes from within. Avoiding disqualification comes from being internally motivated by the power of the Holy Spirit.

The Christian life will become a boring drudgery if we are lacking the essential ingredient of passion.

Passion will get you doing all kinds of things that you never imagined you'd be doing! A good example of this is my husband Nick and how he behaved when we began dating. Nick would sit through chick flicks with me just so he could be with me. (It's funny how he encourages me to go and see similar movies with my girlfriends for a bit of "girl time" now that I am married to him!) He would do anything to be with me when we were dating. He once sat on the beach with me for hours on end. Because I have Mediterranean skin, this didn't bother me in the slightest, but Nick has what I call "English" skin – the type that almost glows in the dark – and so he got a severe sunburn! Why would anyone do that? It has to be because of passion! People will even endure physical pain because of passion. No one forced Nick to watch a movie or to sit in the sun – he did it because he was passionate about me.

Passion will ensure we never run out of steam in our spiritual lives. It is the "inner drive" that will keep our Christian commitment alive, dynamic, vibrant, spontaneous and growing.

Check point 4

Can you remember doing something where you thought, "This is ridiculous!" but you went ahead and did it anyway because you were passionate about it? The German poet Hebbel said,

"Nothing great in the world has even been accomplished without passion." We need to allow the Holy Spirit to kindle the same kind of passion in us. Passion will propel us forward into our destiny.

- Are you increasing in your passion for God and His purpose?
- In what areas of your life can you identify a passion deficiency occurring? How and when did this happen? How do you plan to rekindle this passion?

5. Winners deal with the past

It would be very unwise for any runner to compete while carrying an injury like a stress fracture or a bad muscle sprain. It would seriously limit their ability to run and probably make their condition worse, ultimately taking him or her out of racing for a longer period of time. But there are many Christians who attempt to "run injured" in their spiritual lives. Many are carrying injuries that should have been dealt with and usually this is because they have not addressed issues from their past.

As a young Christian, I had many emotional scars. Although they weren't immediately apparent from the outside, I had a lot of "fault lines" and cracks in my personality that, if not dealt with, I knew would eventually derail me at some point. I had to allow God to deal with those broken areas of my soul or there would be no way that I could finish my course in life. Somewhere along the line, one of those injuries would have flared up and taken me out of the race.

Many people are trying to run their race while suffering from issues such as unforgiveness. They are full of hurt, guilt, anger, shame and bitterness. There is brokenness in their lives that will eventually cause them to fall and end up even more hurt and bitter if they refuse to address it. U2 wrote a song called *Stuck in a Moment You Can't Get Out Of.*[1] It says, "You've got to get yourself together. You got stuck in a moment and now you can't get out of it." There are so many people who have suffered disappointment and hurt in life who are still stuck in that moment. Although they continue to live their lives, a part of them remains in that moment of pain, hurt, abuse, offence or injustice. Sadly, every other experience in their lives is viewed through the filter of that moment.

If we are going to reach forward and take hold of the destiny that God has for us, we cannot stay stuck in a moment of the past. We have to allow the Holy Spirit to do a deep work of healing and restoration in us; to allow Him to go into those wounded, broken places in our souls and mend them so we are not running our race hampered by injury.

We can never move beyond what we are willing to acknowledge in life. If we refuse to admit that we are wounded in a particular area of our lives, it is impossible to deal with it and move on. For instance, there are many people in church life who find it very difficult to submit to authority because of brokenness or perhaps a flawed understanding of the true nature of fatherhood. Others won't fully commit to church life because of abandonment issues in their past. Some won't give financially to the church because they have a poverty mentality, perhaps because they come from a poor background and have a fear of not having enough. Some people don't build healthy emotional attachments because of past abuse or past hurt; and the list goes on.

These people are not enjoying the fullness of all that God has for them in life. They are not running to win and it's not because they don't have the capacity to do it – it is simply because they haven't dealt with issues of the past and they are trying to run with a handicap. We can only do that for so long. A professional athlete, because of years of training and a high level of fitness, can run whilst carrying an injury if he or she has to. But even a professional cannot keep that up for long and would certainly have to bail out of a full-blown competitive race.

By God's grace, I have not only conquered my past, but God is now using my background and my journey to give hope to others who have been abused, marginalised and oppressed. It would have been so easy for me to look at my life and become bitter, disillusioned and crippled by emotional pain, which is what happens when you stay focused on your past.

I could have easily taken on the role of "victim" and blamed everyone else for my condition. But Jesus came into my life and helped me see that I had a life beyond my past. It was this hope of a future that would be different and better than my past that gave me the strength and courage to work through the pain and hurt. It was during this time that I discovered that Jesus did not want me to simply survive my past, but to be "more than a conqueror" (see Romans 8:37). Being more than a conqueror is so much more than fighting and managing to survive. It is about overcoming: being victorious and helping others to win as well.

No matter what pain you are carrying from the past, Jesus can deal with it today. Sins you have committed that you still feel guilty about are gone, once confessed and repented of – history! You can move forward in the grace and acceptance of God. Lingering hurt caused by abuse, betrayal, rejection, can be healed by God's tender touch if you willingly surrender yourself to Him. Don't allow yourself to be bound by the past any longer – with the Holy Spirit's help, move forward and begin running unhindered.

Check point 5

Sometimes in life, we have to look back in order to look forward. Addressing issues from our past that we would rather forget can often be painful, so we tend to avoid doing it; but it is essential that such issues are addressed if we don't want them to trip us up in the future. Ask yourself the following questions:

- Are there areas in my life where pain from the past is still affecting me?
- Is this due to guilt from a past sin that I just need to accept has been forgiven? Or is it due to a particular negative experience?

Depending on how you answer the above questions, you may need to simply pray and ask for God's help, or you may need to ask your church leaders or some close friends to pray with you. Either way, make a commitment to deal with your past and move on.

6. Winners live generously

Any long-distance runner will tell you that a critical factor to going the distance is hydration. If a runner doesn't take on enough water throughout the race, their body will eventually begin to shut down as all of its natural resources are sapped. Water plays a vital role in flushing toxins out of the body and it actually "feeds" our vital organs and helps regulate the temperature of the largest organ of all – our skin. We lose half a litre of water a day just through normal activity, so the more we exercise our body, the more water we need to replace.

Taking on water is a discipline that runners have to observe during a long race even if they don't feel particularly thirsty when they reach a water station. The effects of dehydration can be dramatic and devastating and it can be a problem for even the most experienced runners, let alone inexperienced amateurs. In March 2007 at the 35th IAAF World Cross Country Championships in Mombassa, Kenya, dehydration forced Ethiopian runner Kenenisa Bekele to drop out of the race, and he is the Olympic and World 10,000m Champion. He was also World Cross Country Champion until he forfeited this race.

Describing the effects of dehydration, Bekele said, "It was very difficult. I have never run a race in such difficult conditions ever before in my life ... I did not want to collapse and have people pick me up ... I made a decision to drop out ... from what people tell me I was not conscious when I stopped running. I do not know what might have happened if I had continued running."

Bekele wasn't the only casualty that day. A report on the race said that,

> "The medical tent run by the Coast General Hospital and the Red Cross was a bee-hive of activity and resembled a disaster zone as athlete after athlete was carried in after fainting due to dehydration. Some athletes suffering from effects of excessive heat were put on a drip. At the

finishing line, athletes were dipped in drums of iced water to cool them. Twelve-ton trucks of water were dispatched every half hour or so to replenish the drums! The area resembled the cattle dips found in rural Kenya."[2]

Similarly, "taking on water" in spiritual terms is vitally important to going the distance in our race. We do that by making sure we are constantly refreshing others. Proverbs 11:25 teaches us, *"The generous soul will be made rich, and he who waters will also be watered himself."*

Generosity pertains to every aspect of life. I'm not just talking about money. We can refresh others by being generous towards them with our time, our talents, our possessions, and by learning to put others' needs ahead of our own. If our world is only about "me" and "my needs", we are building a very small world for ourselves. Worse still, we won't be sustained and refreshed by God in the same way that we would if we lived beyond ourselves and learned to "water" the lives of others.

If ever I find that I'm feeling down or weary, or perhaps I'm a bit frustrated because I'm believing God for something that hasn't happened yet, I find the best thing that I can do is to seek to meet someone else's need or to pray for them. Whenever I do, the results are amazing! I've found that as I start to take my eyes off myself and my needs and begin helping others to fulfil theirs, God begins to take care of me and often those deep desires of my heart quickly come to pass.

Even when I was working through the emotional issues of my past and dealing with rejection, unforgiveness, abuse and pain, I found that if I extended my hand to help someone else, my own healing process was accelerated and became much more bearable. God did great things in my life when I took my eyes off myself and focused on the needs of others.

In our ministry, whenever Nick and I have a need, we begin to sow into someone else's need and invariably find that God meets ours. We were recently able to buy some new office premises that we needed because our team had expanded. I believe God blessed us with the funds to do that because we have sought to sow into the needs of others. Whenever we visited other churches around the world, we would always look to sow something into their building fund,

> **I took my eyes off myself and focused on the needs of others.**

believing that God would meet our own needs in His time. We have found without fail that this is a vital key to sustained blessing in our lives.

Check point 6

It's a principle of God that if we live a generous life, we're going to be watered by Him. As we continue to live generously, our world will expand and we will be sustained to run our race to the finish line. Reflect on the following:

- Challenge yourself: am I consumed with my own needs most of the time? If so, what can I do to "water" the lives of those around me?
- Is there a particular need that you've been praying about where the answer has seemed slow in coming? Try seeking to meet someone else's need, believing that God will provide for your need in His time.

7. Winners remain grateful

It is amazing how thankful we are when we first become Christians. We step out of one world and into another and suddenly everything looks great! When I first got saved, every day was an adventure with God and I was grateful for every blessing He sent along. Most new Christians would be the same. They think, "Wow! God is awesome, the church is awesome, the music at church is awesome and so are the people there...!" But, it doesn't seem to take long before all those things that were "awesome" lose their gloss and cynicism and criticism sets in. Why? Because we quickly forget to be thankful.

If we are going to run our race and finish our course, we must keep "an attitude of gratitude" that permeates everything we do. We must ensure that we don't become over-familiar with the goodness of God. We must never develop a sense of familiarity or entitlement which will cause us to lose sight of the finish line.

A lack of gratitude is often the root cause of us getting off track in life. We see this happen in people's marriages. When people first get married they usually act as though their partner is the missing fourth member of the Trinity (especially if they've previously been single for a long time)! But it is amazing how after only a few months, they can become a bit dissatisfied with the very person they prayed so hard that God would give them. It's easy to go from gratitude to familiarity, and from familiarity to disappointment. It is vital to keep nurturing that spirit of thankfulness and allow it to infuse everything we do.

I've discovered that ongoing gratitude makes you whole and keeps your journey fresh. You might think, "But Chris, I've got nothing to be grateful for!" If you know Jesus Christ, then at very least, you can be grateful for the fact that you're not going to hell. If we look hard enough, we will find that there is always something that each of us can be grateful for every day. The choice is ours whether we look at the negative aspects of life or the positive ones. We can choose to be grateful.

For Nick and me, this is non-negotiable in our household. Every day when we pray with our daughters: we thank God that no matter what kind of day we've had, there are things to be grateful for. Sometimes it's just, "God, thank You that I'm still alive!" but we are grateful nonetheless!

Gratitude is so much more than words: it is a heart attitude. I love the story of the ten lepers in Luke 17:11–19. All of these men were healed by Jesus, but only one came back to say "thank you" to Him.

> *"Now it happened as He went to Jerusalem that He passed through the midst of Samaria and Galilee. Then as He entered a certain village, there met Him ten men who were lepers, who stood afar off. And they lifted up their voices and said, 'Jesus, Master, have mercy on us!' So when He saw them, He said to them, 'Go, show yourselves to the priests.' And so it was that as they went, they were cleansed. And one of them, when he saw that he was healed, returned, and with a loud voice glorified God, and fell down on his face at His feet, giving Him thanks. And he was a Samaritan. So Jesus answered and said, 'Were there not ten cleansed? But where are the nine? Were there not any found who returned to give glory to God except this foreigner?' And He said to him, 'Arise, go your way. Your faith has made you well.'"*

> **Gratitude is so much more than words: it is a heart attitude.**

The King James Version translates the last verse, "Your faith has made you *whole*." This story underscores the importance of gratitude when it comes to our wholeness. There are many believers who have been healed, but who are not "whole". They are not whole because they are not grateful. When this man realised that he had been made well by Jesus, he turned around and went back to thank Him. Gratitude is about revisiting "the scene of the event" and acknowledging what happened and Who made it happen. We have good reason to look back and acknowledge the goodness of God in our lives and thank Him for the numerous ways in which He has intervened and blessed us.

Gratitude is a continuous discipline. The fact that nine of the lepers did not come back to personally thank Jesus tells me that thankfulness is not necessarily a natural or instinctive thing. We have to learn to cultivate an attitude of gratitude by making a conscious decision to do so. Rather than focusing on what we don't have, let's stay thankful for what we do have. Let's remember to stay grateful to the One who is making us whole. Gratitude will help take us to our finish line.

Check point 7

When we first become Christians, we are grateful to God for His grace and mercy and an attitude of thankfulness is easy to maintain. As we continue to walk with God gratitude has to be cultivated as a discipline. Reflect on the following truths:

- Every day there is something we can be thankful for.
- Gratitude is a choice!
- Thankfulness is an attitude that can help keep us whole. Make a conscious decision to thank God whenever He intervenes in your life.

8. Winners always get back up

I've left this principle until last because it is one of the great keys to running our race and finishing our course. At times, it is inevitable that we will make mistakes, stumble and fall (unless of course you are perfect!). This in itself does not disqualify us from running our race. Some people, however, make the mistake of not getting back up and continuing to run.

If you trip and fall in a race, you are not disqualified. You are only out of the race if you don't get back up and carry on! One of the greatest schemes of the enemy is to fool us into thinking that we are disqualified because we've fallen; no longer fit to run in God's race. Wrong! I've discovered that God's grace is a lot more expansive than most of us realise. God never gives up on us. He is the God of the second chance, the third chance, the fourth chance, and so on. There is *always* another chance with God (at least on this side of eternity!).

> **God never gives up on us.**

It would be foolish to think that there are no consequences for our actions in life: of course there are. But we can still finish our race no matter what mistakes we have made before. We may feel guilty and ashamed about things that we have done in the past, but that guilt and shame can be dealt with if we bring our sins to Jesus and repent. The Bible teaches us that if we confess our sins, He is faithful and just to forgive us our sins and cleanse us from *all* unrighteousness (1 John 1:9).

The story of King David in 2 Samuel chapter 11 shows us how even the godliest, most passionate believer in God can make a terrible mistake. And it also shows us how, although our actions are bound to have consequences, God's grace is sufficient to restore us and bring us to wholeness.

David is known in Scripture as "a man after God's own heart", but he took a breather and got sloppy.

It started with a lustful look and ended up with a national scandal. He committed adultery with a woman called Bathsheba and had her husband killed so that no one would stand in the way of their affair. David was about fifty years old at the time. He had been ruling the nation successfully for almost twenty years and had distinguished himself as a man of God, a great musician, a poet, a writer and a warrior. Things were going great, but David became complacent. His nation was at war, but instead of being where a king should be (i.e. out leading his troops and urging them to victory), he was kicking back and relaxing. This sometimes happens to us: we have been running our race, doing well for a long time, and we begin to relax. We let down our spiritual guard and we have fallen flat on our face before we know it.

David's adultery had terrible consequences. It led to murder and then the judgement of God which resulted in the death of David's baby son. All of this brought David back to his senses and he repented, asking God for forgiveness. In similar circumstances, many people would have thought to themselves, "That's it – it's all over for me now. I knew better but I've destroyed my destiny in God." David didn't do that. He got back up, repented, accepted God's forgiveness, carried on and finished the course of his race. He suffered the consequences of his actions, but he *was* able to finish.

You may think you have done something that has disqualified you from achieving God's purposes for your life, but I want to tell you this: God never gives up on you! If you feel like that today, *get back up!* You may feel battered and bruised by what has happened in your life, but the Holy Spirit will empower you to stay on track and complete your course as you return to the race. It is God's will for you to run to win in the race of life. He doesn't want you to be disqualified. He has set you up to win and applying the principles that we have learnt will ensure you stay on track and finish strong. You will get your prize at the end of the race, in Jesus' name.

Check point 8

Falling down during your race may be a mistake, but not getting back up and carrying on is a bigger mistake. We often feel so bad when we mess up through sin that we continue to focus on our failure while God is saying, "I've forgiven you, now get up and run!" At other times, life's circumstances will seem to conspire to put us down – these are the times when we just need to get up and keep going.

- You may have stumbled and fallen, but you are not out of the race unless you continue to lie on the floor. Get up and run again!
- No matter what issue in your life has caused you to feel disqualified, God is bigger than the issue!

Part 3 Runners Checklist

Reflect on the lessons learned during this last section of the book.

Along with the determination to win and a commitment to live a different lifestyle, runners have to be skilled in the art of running.

There are eight principles that are pivotal in helping us to keep running strong and avoid disqualification. Most of these principles are simple yet profound; they are spiritual common sense, but incredibly effective if applied consistently.

- Winners obey God's rules
- Winners fix their eyes on Jesus
- Winners learn to love self-control
- Winners stay passionate
- Winners deal with the past
- Winners live generously
- Winners remain grateful
- Winners always get back up

Notes

1. *Stuck in a Moment You Can't Get Out Of,* lyrics by U2/Bono and The Edge, from the album *All That You Can't Leave Behind,* Island Records, 2000.
2. *Source:* G21.net magazine article by Moraa Gitaa.

Conclusion

A designated lane

Each one of us has a "lane" designated to us by God, in which we are to run our race of life. Ephesians 2:10 confirms the uniqueness of each person's individual path: *"For we are His workmanship, created in Christ Jesus for good works, which God prepared beforehand that we should walk in them."*

God had a plan for our lives even before we were born. He had a lane marked out on the track of life with our name on it and a specific race for us to run. God has plucked each one of us out of eternity, positioned us in a certain place in time and given us special gifts and talents for the purpose of serving our generation. There are certain things He wants us to achieve while we are on this side of eternity; primarily the evangelization of planet earth before the second coming of Jesus Christ.

When you and I stand before God one day, we will have to give an account of what we did with our lives. God is going to want to know what we did with the time He gave us, what we did with the talents He gave us and what we did with the treasure He placed in our hands. 2 Corinthians 5:10 says, *"For we must all appear before the judgment seat of Christ, so that each one may be recompensed for his deeds in the body, according to what he has done, whether good or bad"* (NASB).

It is vital that we remember this! We know that we are saved by grace and can do nothing to earn God's free gift of salvation, but the quality of our service here on earth will determine our position and the reward we will receive in heaven. Christians sometimes forget that we will be rewarded on the other side of eternity based on what we have done on this side of eternity. None of us are going to have to give an account of anybody else's race, just our own.

Ask yourself now: where are you in your race of life? Are you in your lane running your race, pressing on for the prize that God has for you? Or are you crawling along somewhere, stumbling and tripping, not really knowing where you're going? Perhaps you are running in your lane of life but you keep looking over to see how others are doing, envying their race and their lane? Or maybe you've collapsed somewhere along the way, become discouraged, disillusioned or disappointed, and you've stopped running? Worse still, perhaps you've become a spectator who sits in grandstand watching the very race you should be running in!

Whatever your assessment of your current race position, I want to encourage you to get up and keep running. Get into your lane, get your head down and run your race to finish your course. No matter how you feel today, know that God has a plan for your life, a unique purpose and destiny only for you. God does not want you to be disqualified. You *can* run your race and finish your course, so run to win!

About the author

A sought after speaker around the world, Christine Caine is passionate about reaching the lost, influencing emerging cultures, inspiring change, strengthening leadership and building the local church. Together with her husband Nick she is part of the leadership team at Hillsong Church in Sydney, Australia, and a director of Equip & Empower Ministries. She lives her life to the full as a wife, teacher, preacher, author and mother of two beautiful daughters, Catherine and Sophia. When the family isn't changing the world on the road they make their home in Sydney, Australia.

Other books by Christine Caine

I'm Not Who I Thought I Was (Equip and Empower)

Youth Ministry – Leading the Next Generation
(Equip and Empower)

A Life Unleashed – Giving Birth to Your Dreams
(Equip and Empower)

Stop Acting Like a Christian ... Just Be One (Regal)

We hope you enjoyed reading this New Wine book.
For details of other New Wine books
and a range of 2,000 titles from other
Word and Spirit publishers visit our website:
www.newwineministries.co.uk